CHILDREN IN WORSHIP:
Lessons from Research

SHIRLEY K. MORGENTHALER

PETER M. BECKER

GARY L. BERTELS

D1496201

PILLARS
PRESS

A division of Concordia University, River Forest

Published in the United States by Pillars Press
The publishing division of Concordia University, River Forest
7400 Augusta Street, River Forest, IL 60305
E-mail: pillarspress@curf.edu; 708-209-3173

Cover design by Carla Sonheim

Library of Congress Cataloging-in-Publication Data applied for.

Printed in the United States of America

To the memory of Peter M. Becker,

whose vision, administrative skill,

and research capacity have been key to the

completion of this study.

TABLE OF CONTENTS

Acknowledgements   vii

Foreword   ix
    Shirley K. Morgenthaler

List of Tables   xi

Chapter One
        Studying Children in Worship   1
            Peter M. Becker

Chapter Two
        Analyzing the Environment   13
            Shirley K. Morgenthaler

Chapter Three
        Analyzing the Communal Rites   27
            Gary L. Bertels

Chapter Four
        Planning from a Child's Perspective   39
            Peter M. Becker

Chapter Five
        Lessons from Research   51
            Shirley K. Morgenthaler

Afterword   63
    Gary L. Bertels

References   65

Appendix A   67
    List of Congregations

Appendix B   75
    Environment Checklist

Appendix C   79
    Worship Checklist

Appendix D   85
    Professional Worker Questionnaire

ACKNOWLEDGMENTS

As with all work which finally reaches completion, the research reported in this book would not have been possible without the support and contributions of many individuals. We are indebted to the administration of Concordia University, River Forest, for its support of the development of the Center for the Study of Children's Ethical Development (CenSCED), under which the work of the *Children in Worship* research has been able to flourish. We are grateful for the input of the participants and presenters at the CenSCED research symposia held in 1992 and 1993. These symposia provided the theoretical and philosophical foundation for the work of *Children in Worship (CIW)*.

Funding for *CIW* has come from the Siebert Lutheran Foundation, Inc. in Wisconsin. The vision of Ronald Jones, President of Siebert, has been an important blessing and foundation for the implementation of this study. The support of the entire Siebert board, and their generous funding, has allowed the research to be conducted. Their foresight in also funding dissemination of the results has allowed this book to be published.

The researchers involved in *CIW* across the country have been key to the success of this endeavor. For this work, the leadership of the various research associates at each of the Concordias in the Concordia University System was essential. These researchers were Marvin Bergman, Jeffrey Burkart, LuJuana Butts, Judith Christian, Sandra Doering, Patricia Hoffman, Gene Ladendorf, John Oberdeck, Lawrence Sohn, Ingeborg Teske, Dennis Verseman, and Richard Wismar. Their guidance of the research assistants who made the multiple visits to the congregations included in the study was central to the quality of the data collected. For this we thank them.

CIW Study One was indeed a team effort, with Associate Directors Gary L. Bertels and the late Peter M. Becker serving as integral to the work of the Project Director. The research staff, as with any multifaceted project, provided the backbone for the work to be done. Elizabeth M. Becker, Concordia University Research and Evaluation Services (CURES) Research Associate, was especially influential in her quiet and competent support of the many details which needed attention. In addition, Jenni Dzurbala, graduate assistant to Study One, brought an enthusiasm and adeptness to her work which greatly impacted the progress of the study.

The opportunity to publish articles in the Lutheran Education journal provided an impetus to the completion of the initial analysis of data. Editor Jonathan Barz deserves our thanks for his support. Finally, the interest of faculty colleagues and church professionals across the country have made the completion of this study and this report fulfilling.

Shirley K. Morgenthaler
Children in Worship Project Director

FOREWORD

The lessons from research reported in this volume have been learned over the past three years in the work on Study One of the *Children in Worship* *(CIW)* research project. Through the generous funding of the Siebert Lutheran Foundation, Inc. of Wauwatosa, Wisconsin, this research has been conducted nationally across the three major Lutheran church bodies in the United States.

The work began as a dream of many people, most notably those individuals who met in 1991 to discuss the possible formation of a new research center at Concordia University in River Forest, Illinois. This research center has been designed to focus on the exploration of issues related to the spiritual and ethical development of children. CenSCED, the Center for the Study of Children's Ethical Development, was formed under the leadership of Dr. William Lehmann Jr., with the assistance of Drs. Gary L. Bertels, the late Peter M. Becker, and Shirley K. Morgenthaler.

Dreaming no small dreams, this team planned and hosted two research symposia which have since resulted in the publication of a book, *Exploring children's spiritual formation: Foundational issues.* This volume has marked not only the initial publication of CenSCED, but also the debut of Pillars Press, the new publishing division of Concordia University, River Forest, Illinois.

As the current director of CenSCED, I have continued in the tradition of the founding director, Dr. Lehmann, to explore issues of importance to the church and to society regarding the spiritual and ethical development of children. The CIW project was developed as an outgrowth of the research symposia, taking its focus from a recurring concern of the participants of those symposia. Children and their understanding of congregational worship have provided the context for Study One of the *Children in Worship* project.

The inclusion of researchers at sister institutions of the Concordia University System has allowed the research to become national in scope. This has allowed the study to indeed become an exploration of the current status of children in worship in Lutheran churches of The Lutheran Church–Missouri Synod, the Evangelical Lutheran Church in America, and the Wisconsin Evangelical Lutheran Synod. Congregations were selected according to a variety of guidelines, including congregational size, community size, age of the congregation, liturgical style, to name a few of the criteria. While the study cannot and does not claim to contain a representative sampling of the church bodies included, it is a beginning attempt to describe the current "state of worship" as it may be perceived by the children participating in that worship.

This book is offered to the reader as a summary of the research it reports. Additional exploration of the data is still needed. This initial attempt to describe what children may "get out of" worship is offered to parents and all those charged with the spiritual formation of children. May it be instructive and motivating toward an ever increasing concern for and sensitivity to the spiritual welfare of the children gifted to us by God.

Shirley K. Morgenthaler
July 1999

LIST OF TABLES

Table One   16
    Architectural Elements in Churches

Table Two   17
    Special Accommodations for Children

Table Three   18
    Presence of Iconic Representations

Table Four   19
    Ecclesiastical Vestments of Clergy

Table Five   20
    Content of Iconic Representations

Table Six   21
    Worship Appointments

Table Seven   22
    Presence of Other Sensory Elements

Table Eight   31
    Children's Inclusion in Ceremonial Acts

Table Nine   32
    Percent Participation by Congregation Members

Table Ten   34
    Frequency of Liturgical Elements in
    Communion Worship Services

Table Eleven   40
    Additional Worship Planners by Denomination

Table Twelve   40
    Additional Planners by Presence of Schools
    and/or Early Childhood Centers

Table Thirteen   41
    Importance of the Child's Perspective to
    Respondent by Denomination

Table Fourteen   42
    Importance of the Child's Perspective to Respondent
    by Presence of School and/or Early Childhood Center

Table Fifteen   43
    Evidence of Inclusion of Children's Perspective
    by Denomination

Table Sixteen   44
    Evidence of Inclusion by Presence of School
    and/or Early Childhood Center

Table Seventeen   45
    Participation in Typical Services by Children under Eighteen

Table Eighteen   45
    Children Under Eighteen Never Participating
    by Denomination

Table Nineteen   46
    Under Eighteen Non-Participation by Presence
    of School and/or ECC

Table Twenty   47
    Children's Involvement in Special Services

Table Twenty-One   48
    School Children's Involvement in Worship

Table Twenty-Two   49
    School Children's Involvement in Worship by
    Denomination—At Least Monthly

CHAPTER 1

Studying Children
in Worship

Peter M. Becker

The *Children in Worship* research has had its beginnings in the Center for the Study of Children's Ethical Development (CenSCED) at Concordia University, River Forest, Illinois. Based on the perceived need for research on children's ethical and spiritual development, Dr. William Lehmann Jr., as the Center's founding director, obtained initial funding for the beginning of CenSCED from the Mary Donnelley Foundation and an anonymous donor. The first activities of the Center were two research symposia which explored a wide variety of theoretical bases for the development of children's spirituality. These symposia attempted to explore and explain the processes of children's moral, ethical, and/or spiritual development. The proceedings of these research symposia have been transformed into a book, *Exploring children's spiritual formation: Foundational issues*, Morgenthaler (1999). This book has been published by Pillars Press and is available from the Concordia University Bookstore, River Forest, Illinois.

The Children in Worship Project

Following the success of the research symposia, the CenSCED associates turned their attention to identifying and developing a project which would build from the findings and implications of the research symposia. One of the theorists whose work had been cited several times during the research symposia was John Westerhoff. His work appeared to the CenSCED research team to be germane to their concerns related to the study of children's spirituality. His theory, more than others, had aspects which could be applied specifically to the spiritual formation of young children.

The analysis of his theory in terms of researchable concepts and constructs led to the development of the *Children in Worship* study. The formative nature of worship appeared to be a rich field of inquiry to test Westerhoff's theoretical perspective. Westerhoff (1992) postulates that the formation of faith takes place among role models with the presence of ritual and predictability, among other factors. Thus, the research team concluded, formation of faith may take place most powerfully in the context of the body of believers and its role modeling for young children in formation. Furthermore, if role models and context are important formative factors, then worship, the most public and common gathering of believers, ought to be a place to examine and operationalize the ideas of John Westerhoff.

Worship, the team concluded, could be studied as an important source for a child's initial moral, ethical, and spiritual development. The research team found, however, that very little research had been conducted on worship practice from a child's perspective. As a result, CenSCED has launched a multiphase research project entitled the *Children in Worship Project (CIW). CIW* is focusing on the formative aspects of a child's worship experience and the impact of corporate worship on a child's spiritual development. John Westerhoff's developmental approach to religious belief and practices is central, theoretically, to the design of the research.

Design of CIW Study One

The study design is intended to examine key aspects of worship in Lutheran churches from the "eyes of a child." Three phases were planned for this research project. These include:

- An initial researchers' conference
- Training of Project Associates and Assistants, and data collection
- Analysis and dissemination

All three phases of Study One were funded by the Siebert Lutheran Foundation of Milwaukee, Wisconsin. To begin the study, an initial researchers' conference was held in September 1995 at Concordia University, River Forest. Participants included educators, musicians, psychologists, and theologians from the ten institutions of the Concordia University System (CUS), representatives of national Lutheran church bodies and the project staff. At the conclusion of the Conference, participants were invited to join in the research effort as Project Associates. Eleven of those present volunteered to participate in Study One of the CIW Project. Each Associate was asked to visit at least one congregation personally. In addition, they were asked to recruit and train three Project Assistants from their institutions who would each visit three congregations. A national sample of congregations from the three major Lutheran denominations was selected, including those which had early childhood centers and/or elementary schools.

A videotape was developed to standardize the training of Project Assistants by the Project Associates. The videotape focused on the use of three instruments which had been developed and field-tested by the CenSCED Associates. These instruments were:

- *CIW* Worship Environment Checklist
- *CIW* Worship Practice Checklist
- *CIW* Professional Worker Questionnaire

The data collection work of the study was conducted in 1996 at eleven locations across the United States. One hundred Lutheran churches were visited on three consecutive Sundays, during which time worship services were observed, the physical environment analyzed, and the worship planner interviewed.

The locations of the eleven Project Associates were used as focal points for the selection of the congregations to be used in the study. The areas in and around the following locations were used:

- Austin, Texas
- Chicago, Illinois
- Seward, Nebraska
- Portland, Oregon
- Irvine, California
- St. Louis, Missouri
- Ann Arbor, Michigan
- St. Paul, Minnesota
- Bronxville, New York (New York City)
- Selma, Alabama
- Mequon, Wisconsin (Milwaukee)

The completed instruments were sent to CenSCED where they were entered into a database. After data cleaning, SPSS programs were developed for each of the instruments. The responses to open-ended questions were also added to the study's databases. Worship folders have also been cataloged for future analysis. The Study's Graduate Assistant, Jennifer Dzurbala, was an integral part of the team for this work.

Initial Analysis

This study was unique in its approach to data analysis. The Project Associates who had overseen data collection in the eleven locations were invited to an analysis conference to begin the interpretation of the initial findings. The core CenSCED team conducted its initial analysis in early 1997. The Project Associates who had led data collection at the outlying sites joined the CenSCED team at an analysis session in April 1997. This meeting involved studying the frequency runs of the three instruments and noting initial reactions to the data. Members of the core CenSCED team led the discussion and analysis for the various sections. The insights, interpretations, and explanations of what was uncovered in the various locations were shared and have helped to shape future analysis of the data.

The highlights of findings and interpretations from the initial analysis then formed the foundation for the in-depth analysis of the results of each of the instruments used in the study. The following highlights summarize the findings from the initial analysis and the Project Associates' analysis meeting.

Demographics

One hundred congregations were included in the final data set of congregations in the CIW research of Study One. These one hundred congregations were a subset of those congregations initially selected for inclusion in the study (see Appendix A). Congregations on this list which were not included in the study were either not visited by a researcher, or data were not judged complete enough for inclusion.

Congregations

- 62 Lutheran Church—Missouri Synod (LCMS)
- 27 Evangelical Lutheran Church in America (ELCA)
- 11 Wisconsin Evangelical Lutheran Synod (WELS)

Worship Style

- 5% High Liturgical
- 38% Traditional
- 43% Blended
- 10% Contemporary

Schools/Early Childhood Centers (ECC)

- 9% School Only
- 40% Both School and ECC
- 17% ECC Only
- 34% Neither/Missing

The initial goal of the study was to select a sample of LCMS, ELCA, and WELS congregations in a six/three/one ratio. It was gratifying to note that the demographics of the completed data collection sites matched that six/three/one ratio very closely. Further, the research team had hoped to find a diversity of worship styles among the sample congregations. This, too, was accomplished. Finally, since full-time educational agencies are important particularly within both LCMS and WELS church bodies, the research team was pleased to see that the sample demographics approximated the goal of a 50% sampling of congregations with schools.

Environment Checklist

Westerhoff's theory includes a focus on the importance of context in the faith formation of young children. The Environmental Checklist was designed to look at the physical settings, or contexts, in which worship was conducted. Bertels and Morgenthaler were especially concerned regarding the impact of imagery and iconic representations on children's development of religious understandings. In addition, however, the research team was also concerned with getting a "feel" for the types of settings that exist in current Lutheran congregations. Initial analysis of the checklists revealed these highlights:

- Exterior access for children to worship spaces was high.
- Interior access for children to the sanctuary was quite good.
- Iconic representations are less present than hoped by the research team.
- There were few special arrangements (such as booster seats) for young children.

- Up to 10% did not have a crucifix or cross in the sanctuary.
- There was very little use of scents or presence of aromas in the churches.
- Most congregations had no reserved areas for families.
- Those congregations that reserved family seating tended to reserve pews in the rear of the sanctuary.

The results of the data appear to indicate that physical settings for worship are planned by adults for adults and not for children. For example, most had single level floors, which means that younger children have a view blocked by adult backs. Only two congregations had booster seats such as those found in every fast food restaurant. Only four churches reserved family seating in the front.

Finally, the richness of iconic representations that might be found in historic churches was lacking in many of the churches sampled. Yet, to children who do not read, those iconic representations are visual images which have important nonverbal teaching impacts.

Worship Checklist

Another important aspect of faith formation, according to Westerhoff, is the presence of ritual and predictability. The Worship Checklist was designed to measure the presence or absence of various liturgical elements—ritual and predictability—in worship services. The Associates and Assistants were asked to observe three consecutive Sunday worship sessions in a church. This was designed so that one could determine what are "typical" as opposed to "special" worship experiences of children. Preliminary findings indicate that:

- Children participate more if the congregation operates a school or an early childhood center.
- Older children (age 12 and above) as acolytes (60%) are the most prevalent children's involvement in congregational worship.
- The children's message is a common form of including children in worship (40%).

- Participation in children's choir (30%) is another frequent form of involvement.
- Children of the congregation are brought to communion with their parents more often than they are invited forward to witness a baptism.
- Participation of lay members of the congregation is limited. Lay readers are the highest frequency of participation at 50% of congregations.
- Many congregations limit children's participation to special services such as Christmas.
- Communion services are different from non-communion.
- Some "traditional" liturgical elements are missing in the worship of many congregations.

For most children, worship is a "spectator" activity. Worship is done by adults for adults. Older children can light candles; younger children can come forward for "their" message; and they can "perform" at holidays. But, on most Sundays children can "watch," if they can find a sight line. Liturgies, which contain elements that often need to be explained to children, vary so frequently children may not ever find a pattern. This lack of a pattern may delay formative acquisition of the ritual of the worship experience. Finally, the "majesty" of the worship liturgy which some adults have found highly formative is less present than expected.

Worship Planner Interview

A third element of Westerhoff's theory is the intentionality of adults in the "enculturation" of young children and new Christians into the community of believers. Thus, the final instrument used was an interview schedule designed to gain the perspective of the person who did the worship planning for the congregation. Questions regarding that individual's understanding of children's role and perspective in worship were asked. Following are some of the highlighted preliminary findings.

- The pastor or senior pastor most frequently plans worship (85%).
- Children's perspectives in that planning were considered "very

important" by 33% of planners, "somewhat important" by 55%, and "slightly important" or "not important" by 11% of those participating in the interview.

- Children's perspectives were judged to be "very important" to congregation members 26% of the time. Children's perspectives were perceived to be "somewhat important" 53% of the time, and "slightly" or "not important" 21% of the time.
- Inclusion of a children's sermon was cited as the most popular method of planning for and involving children.
- A communion blessing also cited as a way of involving children in worship.

It is clear that some recognition of children's presence in worship is present among those who plan worship. However, it is limited to special events: children's sermons, joining parents during communion or a baptism, or special services on holidays.

Children enter the consideration of the worship planner only slightly more than that person perceives their importance to the membership. The participants at the initial analysis conference suggested that the high response to considering children's perspectives "somewhat important" really is the "politically correct" answer. Their impression was that the actual valuing of children's perspectives in the planning of worship was lower than that. There is some evidence that children are more salient to worship planning in those churches with schools and/or early childhood centers.

Future Data Reports

The reflections in this chapter reveal initial reactions to the findings from the three instruments used in the CIW study. They summarize initial data analysis. The research team, especially the principal researchers, then studied each of the instrument results in greater depth. Those results, then are reported in the subsequent chapters of this book. These chapters explore each set of data in turn.

While the data being reported are for Lutherans in general, there is some evidence that differences exist between church bodies, as well as between congregations with and without schools and early childhood centers. Additional data collection will allow the researchers to verify these perceptions. CenSCED Associates also hope to have interested parties in other traditions use the instruments and share comparative data. This will allow the researchers to expand interpretation of the data in general and to develop additional inferences and conclusions.

The first full phase of analysis was completed by the research team at CenSCED. In addition, each of the Project Associates has received access to the data bases so that they may pursue their individual research interests. It is the hope of the CenSCED team that they will also share the data bases with their students to expand the analyses undertaken.

Future CIW Project Studies

The next studies in the *Children in Worship* series are in the planning phase. These studies have grown out of the work of CenSCED's Associates and the *CIW* Project Associates. Identified as Study Two is an observational study focusing on children's actual behavior during worship, including video taping both of the service and of children's behavior during the service. Study Three, which may be combined with Study Two if sufficient funding can be found, will focus on interviews with children to determine their perceptions of—and reactions to—worship.

These two studies are planned as preliminary strategies to assess which activities children find meaningful and worshipful from their own perspective, rather than from adults' interpretations of their perspectives.

Concluding Comments

Study One of the *Children in Worship* project has received initial analysis. Each of the three CenSCED team members at Concordia has taken the lead in analysis of the data in one of the instruments. Interest in the findings has already been expressed by musicians, educators, and synodical staffs of the three Lutheran bodies. Several researchers have expressed interest in replicating the study in other denominational settings.

The research team has received preliminary funding to plan Studies Two and Three. In addition, replications of Study One across denominations are objects of potential funding to be sought.

CHAPTER 2

Analyzing
the Enviornment

Shirley K. Morgenthaler

For all young children, learning is a total and sensory experience (Piaget, 1955). They learn through all of their senses simultaneously. They take in the sights and sounds, smells and tastes, as they take in the whole of a new experience. Who has not seen an infant look at a new object, such as a rattle or soft toy, and almost instantaneously watched that object be put into the mouth for further investigation?

Such total investigation takes place in worship as well. Young children apprehend worship through all of their senses–smell and touch and even taste, as well as sight and hearing. It is only as Christians begin to understand the comprehensive nature of this experience that they will analyze what they are providing for the very young in their midst (Westerhoff, 1992).

One aspect of the *Children in Worship* (CIW) Study One was the analysis of the environment in the 100 congregations visited across the United States by the CIW team. This chapter reports the research team's analysis of what currently exists environmentally in churches of the Lutheran

Church–Missouri Synod (LCMS), the Evangelical Lutheran Church in America (ELCA), and the Wisconsin Evangelical Lutheran Synod (WELS).

Theoretical Foundations

For the theoretical base of the *CIW* study, the research team built upon the work of John Westerhoff (1976, 1982, 1992). Westerhoff's theoretical framework of faith formation provided a seminal perspective on the development of the child's understanding of the faith into which he or she has been baptized. Westerhoff (1996) postulates that Christians spend a lifetime "living into" the baptism which began their relationship with God. This faith formation is built upon role modeling, appropriate environments, and the intentionality of experiences provided for children as their understanding of their faith forms (Westerhoff, 1997).

In worship, role modeling is provided for young children as they observe the worship activity of the adults around them. They observe the singing, listening, and praying of their parents and of the other adults important to them. Children also observe the actions and activities of children somewhat older than themselves. They notice whether older children and adolescents are invited to usher, to acolyte, to sing in a choir. They ascertain whether they are able to aspire to similar activities. This aspect of faith formation in worship is more fully explored in the next chapter focusing on the rituals and ritual acts of worship.

The intentionality of experiences provided for children are also important. Children learn most powerfully and effectively when adults provide experiences which take the child's capacity to understand into account. This intentionality of experiences is more fully explored in a subsequent chapter focusing on the perspective of the worship planner in providing for the inclusion of children in worship.

Appropriate worship environments for young children teach children about worship. Are there visual images of faith and faith stories for children to see and study? Are there symbols which depict the key elements of the faith of the worshiping community? Are there objects to touch which tell the faith story? Are there sounds which appeal to and can be understood by young children? Are there smells and aromas which signify "church" and "worship" for the child? Each of the senses can potentially be used by the child to learn more about the faith story of the worshiping community.

Environmental Messages

Church environments which are planned with children in mind will "speak" to the pre-literate child in powerful ways through the visual images of color and symbol. They will also "speak" to the child through auditory messages beyond words, such as through bells, language cadences, loud/soft sounds, etc. Planned environments will also include olfactory messages through things like candles, flowers, and wood. Child-friendly environments will also include a variety of textures which are accessible to children. These may include the smooth and shiny wood of the pew, the soft or nubby fabric of cushions, the softness of a "church book" provided for the very young child.

Environmental messages are also given to the parents and families who bring young children to church. Appointments in the environment may quickly indicate whether young children are even expected to be or to stay in the worship setting. How accessible is the environment for the family with children? Are there items such as booster seats or children's bulletins which would say that young children are expected in this place? How well will children be able to view the activity at and near the altar without obstruction?

While many of the aspects of the environment which were analyzed in the CIW study speak only subtly of the doctrinal position of the church bodies studied, these aspects do powerfully indicate the degree of intentional inclusion of children in the worshiping community. These aspects indicate whether children are expected to learn to worship by worshiping. These aspects also indicate whether worship is considered an adult or an intergenerational activity.

The CIW Environment Checklist

The Environment Checklist of the CIW study (see Appendix B) was one of three tools designed to measure the support of faith formation (Westerhoff,

1992) which was present in the corporate worship of the 100 congregations included in the study. The results of the Worship Checklist and the Professional Worker Questionnaire will be reported in the next chapters.

The Environment Checklist consisted of three major sections: architecture, sensory elements, and accommodations. The 100 congregations included in the study were asked to identify their style of worship. The styles reported were "liturgical," "traditional," "blended," "mixed," "contemporary," and "informal." These self-reported styles were then used as one set of independent variables in analyzing the data.

Architecture

In most congregations, both interior and exterior access for families with young children was quite good. Overall, researchers found the church buildings to be warm rather than cold, accessible rather than inaccessible. Table One lists the architectural elements present in the 100 congregations observed in that study. The checklist also asked researchers to note the presence of a communion rail (87%), pulpit (90%), lectern (82%), altar (99%), and baptismal font (92%).

Communion rail	87%
Pulpit	90%
Lectern	82%
Altar	99%
Baptismal font	92%
Place to walk with restless toddler	35%
N = 100	

Table One. Architectural Elements in Churches

A question on the environment observation tool asked the observer to determine whether the church being observed had a place to walk with restless toddlers. This was defined to be an area which did not take the adult and toddler totally out of the worship setting. Of the congregations included in the study, 35 had such an area in the worship environment. Blended and mixed worship styles were more likely than traditional worship styles to have places to walk with restless toddlers.

Accommodations

Special arrangements for families with young children were rare in the churches sampled. Only two of the one hundred congregations supplied booster seats for young children in an attempt to give young children greater visual access to the worship activities.

Booster seats	2%
Reserved seating	
Front pews	4%
Rear pews	19%
None	67%
N= 100	

Table Two. Special Accommodations for Children

One of the two congregations which supply booster seats has both an early childhood center and a school; the other has neither. Interestingly, both congregations which supplied booster seats for young children reported using a traditional worship style.

Most congregations (69%) did not reserve seating areas for families. However, of those that did reserve seating areas, five times as many congregations (19%) reserved pews in the rear of the church rather than pews in the front of the church (4%). Again, visual access for children did not appear to be a prominent consideration for worship in most congregations.

Those places with front pews reserved for families have either traditional or blended worship styles. Three of the congregations reserving front pews have an early childhood education center or program. Only one of those congregations had neither an early childhood education center nor a school.

None of the congregations with a school only (and no early childhood program) reserved front pews. It is interesting to note that none of the congregations who described their worship style as contemporary or informal reserved back pews for families with young children.

Members of the research team were also asked to record the presence and use of kneelers in the congregations they visited. Congregations describing themselves as traditional or blended in worship style had the majority of kneelers (54%). These congregations also were more likely to have an early childhood center (35%) or both an early childhood education center and a school (28%).

Visual elements

Iconic representations (stained glass windows, banners, murals, pictures, statuary, and symbols of key elements of the faith) were less present than hoped by the research team. The evaluation of iconic representations included an evaluation of their prominence and the height placement of pictures, banners, and symbols so as to make them visually accessible for young children. Of the congregations who did have iconic representations, 60% had them "easily viewable" by children.

Stained Glass	77%
Murals	11%
Statues	28%
Pictures/paintings	28%
Banners	
Words	17%
Words and symbols	66%
Symbols and pictures	50%
N = 85	

Table Three. Presence of Iconic Representations

Churches and congregations that defined their worship style as liturgical, traditional or blended were more likely to have stained glass in the worship environment (77%). At the same time, these liturgical or traditional environments were less likely to have murals (11%), statues (28%), or pictures/paintings (28%) in the worship environment. Congregations with early childhood centers and/or schools (45%) were also more likely to have stained glass in the worship environment. Murals were somewhat more likely to be present (30%) in congregations with both early childhood centers and schools.

Pictures and paintings were somewhat more likely to be present in the worship setting in those congregations describing their worship as mixed or informal (36% and 50%). These same congregations were most likely to have both an early childhood center and a school (43%).

In those 64 congregations including banners in the worship setting, those banners were most likely to have a combination of words and symbols (81%). Banners were most likely to be present in congregations describing their worship style as blended or mixed (81%). Banners also were more likely to be present in congregations with early childhood centers (73%).

Members of the research team were also asked to note the presence of statues in the worship environment. The presence of statues was more likely in those congregations describing their worship as blended (26%) or informal (50%). These same congregations were most likely to have a school or a school and an early childhood center (34%).

Chasuble	25%
Alb	71%
Cassock/Surplice	4%
N = 100	

Table Four. Ecclesiastical Vestments of Clergy

Ecclesiastical vestments were considered to be another element of the visual environment for children in worship. Of the vestment options, the chasuble was considered to be the most dramatic of the options. This element was considered most likely to catch the eye of even the very young child in worship. Those congregations describing their worship as liturgical (50%), or traditional (42%) were more likely than other worship styles to use the chasuble as a vestment for worship.

One of the questions asked regarding the environment was the content of the iconics in the worship environment. This content would include those events or concepts depicted in stained glass, the subjects of pictures, paintings and banners, and the types of statuary and symbols present.

Jesus	68%
Trinity	61%
Bible stories	41%
Saints	14%
Nonspecific designs	43%
Abstract art	22%

Table Five. Content of Iconic Representations

The most common content of worship iconics was representations of Jesus (68%). This was somewhat more likely to be present than representations or symbols of the Trinity (61%). Bible stories were less frequently present than depictions of Jesus or the Trinity (41%). Bible stories were more likely to be depicted in the iconics of the worship environment (65%) in settings where a school and/or early childhood center were present. Nonspecific designs (43%) and/or abstract art (22%) were also present but not as commonly as depictions of Jesus, the Trinity, or prominent Bible stories. Depictions of saints (14%) were the least likely content for iconic representations in those worship environments analyzed. In all of the congregations visited, worship style was not a strong indicator for the content of iconics in the worship setting.

Candles	94%
Cross	89%
Baptismal font	96%
N = 100	

Table Six. Worship Appointments

Appointments, such as candles, the cross, and the baptismal font were also noted as elements of the visual environment of the worship setting for children in worship. In those congregations visited, the baptismal font tended to be prominent in all of the congregations. However, the baptismal font tended to be slightly less prominent in those congregations describing their worship style as blended or mixed. In addition, the baptismal font tended to be more prominent in those congregations with early childhood education centers.

Eleven of the congregations sampled did not have a cross in the chancel. It is unclear whether there was a cross in another part of the sanctuary. However, the absence of the chancel cross would mean that children did not have the opportunity to see this important representation of the Christian faith.

Other Sensory Elements

There was very little use of scents or presence of aromas in the churches. In most churches the smell of candles burning was not present even if candles were lit. This appeared to be caused by the use of candela, or oil-burning candles. Thus, for most children, this sensory element was absent. Those congregations which did have moderate candle aroma present were primarily congregations reporting their worship style as traditional or blended.

Incense was present in only one church observed in the study. This congregation reported its worship style as blended and had both an early childhood center and a school. The absence of this sensory element in most of the congregations means that yet another opportunity to include a sensory memory of worship for children was missed.

Morgenthaler

Candles	17%
Incense	1%
Flowers	17%
Wood	22%
N = 98	

Table Seven. Presence of Other Sensory Elements

The smell of flowers in the worship environment was present in only 17% of the congregations. As with the aroma of candles, these congregations described their worship style as either traditional or blended.

The aroma of wood was another sensory element judged by the CIW researchers. This, too, was absent in a majority (78%) of congregations. In those congregations where the smell of wood was judged to be strong or moderate, their worship style had been reported as traditional or blended. The majority of these congregations had both an early childhood center and a school.

Implications and Interpretations

From the data reported above, it is clear that the perspective of children in worship was not strongly considered in the majority of the congregations included in the study. Yet, if Westerhoff's theory (1992, 1996) is valid, these congregations have missed an important opportunity. The opportunity to welcome children into worship begins with small but powerful messages that children are expected to be present. These messages would include where children are expected to be seated if they are to participate, whether special seating accommodations, such as booster chairs for toddlers and preschoolers, are available, and what kinds of other intentional provisions have been made for children and their families.

From the perspective of the environment, welcoming children into worship might mean the inclusion of banners and pictures which represent key stories or tenets of the faith of the congregation. Thus, the presence of representations of Jesus, the Trinity, and prominent Bible stories provide powerful nonverbal teaching for pre-literate young children in the congregation. Just as in the days of Luther and earlier, the use of symbols and pictures could teach concepts and Scriptural truths to those in the congregations for whom words may not be accessible. In earlier days, the issue was illiteracy of adults. While that may not be as serious a problem in churches today, the pre-literacy of young children ought still to be a consideration in the selection of appointments and visual stimuli in the worship setting.

Church leaders, worship planners, and parents all bear responsibility for providing appropriate access for children in the worship setting. Even though reserved seating was not designated in most of the congregations visited, it is probable that parents with young children opted to sit near the back of the church. This may be due, at least in part, to their socialization into the value of not disturbing others, especially those without small children, who are also worshiping. However, it may also be due to the attitudes of others caught through glances or comments in response to the wiggles or noises of young children in worship.

It is important to consider what is being taught by the choice of seating for families with young children. Families who decide to attend the circus or a similar spectator event with young children will opt for the seats closest to the front so that their children may have an unobstructed view. What are these same families saying to their children when they opt for the rear seats in church? Is the child's participation less important in church?

The results of the data appear to indicate that physical settings for worship are planned by adults, for adults and not for children. For example, most had single level floors, which means that younger children have a view blocked by adult backs. For children, especially young children, worship is viewed as primarily a spectator activity. Yet with the blocked view and limited accommodations, children are given very limited opportunity to spectate.

It is incumbent upon church leaders to examine the value for children of corporate worship as it is currently practiced. There are several questions which need to be answered:

- What are the messages being given?
- How are children welcomed into the worshiping community?

- What messages of welcome and expectation are given to parents with young children?
- What accommodations are made for families with young children?
- Are young children being taught to tune out before they have even tuned in?
- What are the messages and evidences of welcome which would tell children and their parents that they are not simply tolerated, but welcomed and provided for?

Each congregation will need to assess its accommodations for and welcoming of children for itself. Each congregation will need to determine if there are practices and attitudes which can be modified in order to move worship for children from a spectator activity to a meaningful experience in which children, too, can celebrate their relationship with God and grow in that relationship.

Congregations also need to assess the power of the iconic representations which are currently found in their worship environments. The researchers have concluded that the majority of the churches sampled did not have the richness of iconics which they had hoped to find. These iconics seem to have been eliminated from newer church buildings, possibly in an effort to economize on costs of construction. However, that cost-cutting may have been accomplished at the expense of providing a rich teaching environment for children in worship. The power of the nonverbal for the pre-reader in providing messages of important and core values of that worshiping community should not be underestimated.

If Westerhoff's theory is correct, as the researchers believe, then Lutheranism must re-examine its worship practices in regard to children. In Westerhoff's theory, children are not to be relegated to a children's church or a developmentally appropriate experience. Rather, they are to be welcomed into a truly intergenerational worship experience in which both the setting and the worship rituals themselves are planned with believers of all ages in mind.

Subsequent chapters in this volume will report on the results of the CIW worship observation and of the CIW worship-planner questionnaire.

These chapters, together with this discussion of the environment, will provide the reader with a full picture of the current status of children in worship. This, then, will give the reader the resources to assess worship practices where he or she is in ministry.

CHAPTER 3

Analyzing the Communal Rights

Gary L. Bertels

John Westerhoff's theory of "faith formation" affords the opportunity for serious reflection on the intersection of theology and the social sciences. This is not a new venture for those involved in religious instruction. Philosophies of Christian education have historically attempted to facilitate a dialogue between theology and psychology, sociology, anthropology, and the other related social sciences. However, Westerhoff's (1996) contention that the heart of "living into" one's baptism is formation, and not instruction or education, presents the challenge of integrating not only one's theology and education, but perhaps what is more important, one's theology of the Church and worship, and the disciplines of the social sciences. It is this challenge of integration which is at the heart of the research involved in the *Children in Worship* study.

Theoretical Foundations

Westerhoff's theory postulates that there are eight aspects of communal life which contribute to and influence the practices and experiences that are necessary for spiritual formation: (1) communal rites; (2) environment; (3) time; (4) communal life; (5) discipline; (6) social interaction; (7) role models; and, (8) language (Westerhoff, 1992). Recognizing that the worship setting is one of the contexts in which many of the eight aspects of formation intersect, the CIW team limited its study to that setting. The previous chapter has addressed the environmental messages of the 100 congregations visited. This chapter will concern itself with the aspect of communal rites. It will attempt to report the team's analysis of what currently exists in the practice of communal rites in sixty-two congregations of the Lutheran Church—Missouri Synod (LCMS), twenty-seven congregations of the Evangelical Lutheran Church in America (ELCA), and eleven congregations of the Wisconsin Evangelical Lutheran Synod (WELS).

Referencing Willard Sperry's *Reality in Worship* (1932), Westerhoff observes that

> the church shares with many other institutions common tasks that are religious in nature, and that many of these activities are done better by institutions other than the church. The one unique contribution of the church is its cultic life. While the work of the church is real and intelligible through the life and actions of its members in daily life, *the church is clearly defined whenever and wherever people meet together to address themselves to the act of liturgy.* (Westerhoff, 1992, p. 272, emphasis the author's)

In discussing cultic life, Westerhoff is referring to "liturgy," a community's rites: "repetitive, symbolic, and social acts which express and manifest the community's sacred narrative, along with its implied faith and life" (Westerhoff, 1992, p. 272). He makes the distinction between "ceremonial acts," which are prescribed behaviors, and "ritual acts," which are prescribed words. Westerhoff maintains that these "liturgies," or community rites, include,

> (1) rites of intensification that follow the calendar (once a week, month, or year) and shape, sustain, and enhance the community's faith, character, and consciousness, as well as increasing group solidarity; (2) rites of transition that follow the life cycle and promote meaningful passage for persons and the community from one stage of life to another; and (3) rites of initiation that induct persons 'into the community.' (Westerhoff, 1992, p. 272)

The CIW Worship Checklist

On three consecutive Sundays, the *Children in Worship* research associates and assistants observed the ceremonial and ritual acts of 100 congregations. This procedure was adopted to measure the presence or absence of various liturgical elements in the worship services, and to determine what were "typical" as opposed to "special" worship experiences of children in those congregations. The Worship Checklist (see Appendix C) was developed to record the presence or absence of the various liturgical elements of worship in each of the 100 congregations and 300 worship services which were included in the study.

Following the observations, the "liturgies" of the communities were grouped according to the proximity of their adherence to the public services published in the hymnals of the three denominations. Five worshiping communities which followed the prescribed ceremonial and ritual acts, and did so in "high church" fashion, were identified as being "liturgical." Twenty-seven communities which followed the prescribed rites without the "high church" fashion, were identified as "traditional." Twenty-two worshiping communities which incorporated elements not reflected in the services found in the hymnal, and/or omitted particular rites from the hymnal order, were identified as "blended." Eleven communities which combined elements from the prescribed orders of worship and other sources and conducted the service in a formal style were identified as "mixed." Nine communities which developed their own worship forms, or which used produced worship forms which did not reflect the orders of worship in the hymnal, were identified as "contemporary." Two worshiping communities which conducted their worship in a less formal style and did not incorporate many prescribed rites, were identified as "informal." Four communities identified themselves as "other."

The research associate's and assistant's judgement and the community's self-labeling were the sole criteria used in grouping the worshiping communities' liturgies. Future data collection may need to incorporate clearer descriptions of worship styles, and will most likely refine the number of groupings. The denomination with the greatest variety of liturgies was the LCMS, with the WELS evidencing the least. The percentage of each denomination represented in the study undoubtedly influenced this finding.

The "Ceremonial Acts" listed on the checklist included various elements which reflected the role or participation of children in worship and the role models offered to them. The list included children's message, children's song, children accompanying parents to the communion rail, children named in prayers, special accommodations for children, and children's and layperson's involvement in worship activities (reading, singing in a choir, ushering, acolyting, etc.).

The "Rituals" listing included such elements as formal processionals, kneeling for confession and/or prayer, standing at the appropriate times, making the sign of the cross, Gospel procession, celebration of Holy Communion, lay reader participants, and use of hymnal, Bible, and/or worship folder.

The "Ritual Acts" listing included the various elements identified in the Service with Holy Communion forms in the three hymnals, with the addition of the tolling of the bell, processional, and recessional.

Findings of the Study

The findings of the observations are limited to the congregations visited, on particular Sundays, for the particular services, and must not be generalized to all worshiping communities. However, the findings may reflect the experiences of children in many Lutheran congregations.

Ceremonial Acts

Ceremonial acts include activities and participation opportunities for children in worship. They also include an identification of role models available to children, especially older children and youth serving as role models. Table Eight summarizes these data.

Children's message	40%
Children's song	20%
Adult leader greeting children	43%
Children accompanying parents to communion	80%
Comments to children during sermon	30%
Children's bulletins	40%
Children's choir	27%
Children assisting in worship	
acolytes	60%
usher	28%
crucifer bearer	6%
instrumentalist	6%
book bearer	2%
banner bearer	2%
N = 100	

Table Eight. Children's Inclusion in Ceremonial Acts

In about 40% of the worship services a children's message was included; 20% of the services included a children's song; 43% of the time an adult leader greeted the children; and, in about 80% of the services the children accompanied their parents to the communion rail during distribution.

Children rarely heard their names spoken during the public worship of their community. The occasion for it being spoken was more likely to be because of sickness or in observance of their birthday rather than in remembrance of their baptism birthday. In 30% of the communities the preacher included comments to the children during the message. Children's bulletins have found their way into approximately 40% of the congregations. On average, a little more than one in four services included children singing in a choir during worship. However, this was the second highest opportunity for children to participate in worship. Sixty percent of the services had children serving as acolytes, the highest occasion of participation of children, while children serve as ushers (28%) much less frequently, crucifer (6%), instrumentalist (6%), book bearer (2%), or banner bearer (2%). It is the position of the researchers that participating older children and youth serve as role models for the younger children, indicating what they someday may be doing as participants in worship.

In comparing congregations with schools and/or early childhood centers with congregations which had neither, one discovers that the level of children's participation increased when a congregation maintained a school or early childhood center. This increased participation was evident in the number of services with children singing in a choir.

Rituals

Rituals are those specific activities or elements found in worship. These are physical actions or expectations included in worship beyond the liturgy itself. Table Nine reports the frequency of selected rituals in worship with communion.

Procession	43%
Kneeling for confession	10%
Making the sign of the cross	9.3%
Lay readers	
male	53%
female	47%
white	90%
black	10%
Eucharist assistants	
white male	94%
N = 100	

Table Nine. Percent Participation by Congregation Members

In communities when holy communion was being celebrated, 43% of the services included in the rituals a procession, many of which included children. In less than 10% of the communities participants knelt for confession or prayer. However, in every community the participants stood at the appropriate times. In less than 10% of the services participants made the sign of the cross at the points indicated in the traditional worship service, or observe a Gospel processional. When lay readers were incorporated into the service, they were generally white males. However, in 47% of the services observed, the lay readers were female, and about 10% of the time the readers were black. Ninety-four percent of the Eucharist assistants were white males.

In more than 50% of the communion services observed, the hymnal was not used as a guide for worship, while in only 20% of the services was it used in reading or chanting the appointed psalm. However, in 80% of the services the hymnal was used for the singing of the hymns. Fourteen percent of the services included using the Catechism portion of the hymnal in worship. Fifty percent of the services included the opportunity to use the pew Bible. Eighty-eight percent of the services included the use of a worship folder.

The following list summarizes the general observations found for worship services when communion was not being celebrated. These observations are made by comparing these worship services to worship with communion.

(1) processionals were less likely to have been observed
(2) kneeling was not a part of the community's rituals in more than 90% of the communities
(3) the pastor was the only one making the sign of the cross in 92% of the communities
(4) the hymnal was used in half of the services as a guide for worship but was used in 75% of the services for singing hymns
(5) the pew Bible was used during less than half of the services
(6) the Catechism portion of the hymnal was referenced in only 15% of the services
(7) more than 80% of the services observed included the use of a worship folder

Ritual Acts

Ritual acts are the elements of the worship liturgy itself as it is outlined and identified in the various Service with Holy Communion forms found in the hymnals of the three denominations studied. In addition, the tolling of the bell, the processional, and the recessional were included as ritual acts.

Table Ten summarizes the average percentages of ritual acts observed in the congregations during a communion service.

During non-communion services the elements listed above that remained at constantly high percentages included: an opening hymn; the

Tolling of the bell	37%
Greeting	95%
Call to Worship	69%
Processional	13%
Opening hymn	96%
Invocation	89%
Confession and Absolution	89%
Entrance rite:	
Introit	36%
Hymn	69%
Kyrie	54%
Hymn of Praise	61%
Collect of the Day	65%
Readings	100%
Psalmody	40%
Sermon	100%
Creed	83%
Offering	100%
Offertory	85%
Preface and Proper Preface	57%
Sanctus	48%
Lord's Prayer	99%
Words of institution	100%
Exchange of Peace:	
Spoken	30%
Hand shake	53%
Agnus Dei	52%
Salutation	60%
Benediction	99%
Closing Hymn	90%
Bell/Chimes	12%

Table Ten. Frequency of Liturgical Elements in Communion Worship Services invocation; confession and absolution; a sermon; a creed; the offering; the benediction; and a closing hymn. It must be noted that these data come from responses on the Worship Checklist itself, and that the non-communion worship folders have not been reviewed for this analysis. The information reflects data reported by the associates and assistants on the checklists.

In reviewing the ritual acts, it becomes apparent that in many worship settings several of the traditional liturgical elements were missing. However, in every setting there were readings, a sermon, singing, and an offering. In reviewing children's participation in ceremonial acts, the most prevalent participation in worship by children was in their serving as acolytes.

Initial Implications

In reviewing Westerhoff's concern for cultic life and the role that community actions play in spiritual formation, it becomes evident that a greater degree of attention must be paid to the experiences of children in worship. It is a marked improvement from the past that in 40% of the services observed a children's message is included. However, in 60% of the congregations in the study, a children's message was not observed. A future area of study may be an examination of the content of children's messages and the children's perceptions of that content. However, regardless of the conclusions of the future study, the children in that 40% doubtless appreciated the fact that they were included in the service, and that special attention was paid to the ones for whom much of worship is observed rather than done. With the increase in the number of children's messages, there is hope that a children's song may someday become a regular part of a community's ceremonial acts. With the dominant role that singing plays in the worship experience, it is imperative that children participate as early and as often as possible.

A ceremonial act that one would expect to observe regularly in the worship life of denomination that practices infant baptism is the celebration of baptism birthdays, at least the inclusion of a prayer of thanksgiving and for preservation and continued protection, along with prayers for the parents and sponsors. The practice of praying for the catechumens may need to be expanded to include all baptized children of the congregation on the occasion of the remembrance of their baptism.

For children, the rituals, or actions of the worshiping body, carry much of the message of the worship experience. Worship postures communicate much about what is going on to the young child; kneeling for confession and prayer, standing for the liturgy and Gospel reading, and sitting for the sermon and most hymns, all communicate appropriate worshipful attitudes that are caught by the child. The noted absence of many of these rituals in many of the communities should be a cause for concern. What attitudes of worship are we teaching when children experience worship as spectators rather than as active participants? The various rituals in liturgical worship afford opportunities for children to catch the wonder and majesty of worship.

Luther's admonition that Christians should make the sign of the cross to remind themselves of their baptism and as a witness to their neighbors should be assessed in light of the fact that in fewer than 10% of the services was this ritual observed.

The increased use of worship folders at the expense of children being introduced to the content and workings of the hymnal may concern some. At one time the hymnal was an artifact of the Christian community that was a pocket-size home devotional resource as well as an aid in corporate worship. Now it is falling into disuse, even in corporate worship. Few communities are introducing their children to the storehouse of devotional materials found in the hymnal. Its use has been relegated to the singing of hymns, and, in some communities, not even that. Less than 14% of the services observed incorporated a portion of the Catechism section of the hymnal in the worship experience. Will children be aware of the Christian Questions and Answers, the daily Bible reading calendar, and the variety of worship and devotion forms found in the hymnal when the hymnal is used primarily for singing? One would hope to see an increase in the use of the Bible during public worship. In more than half of the services observed the Bible was not used. What do these rituals or their absence teach children? How important are these tools of the worshiping community and to the messages that community gives to its children?

In reviewing the findings from the ritual acts section of the checklist (see appendix B) one recognizes that in some communities some elements of the liturgy are also falling into disuse. In some worshiping communities, the name of the Triune God into which the children were baptized is not spoken at the beginning of worship. The absence of the majestic elements of worship such as a processional, Gospel procession, and recessional may contribute to the sense of a lack of celebration that reportedly marks some worship experiences. Often these ritual acts communicate to the children present the glory and majesty of the occasion of worshiping God. Corporate gestures, such as making the sign of the cross and the exchanging of peace before reception of the sacrament also model for children the relationship that exists in the community.

It does appear that there are a few rituals of worship upon which children can always depend. These include Scripture readings, the sermon, and the offering. Are these the primary acts of worship with which we welcome children into the community? Predictability and dependability are two characteristics of a safe and welcoming community. What is the effect upon children when worship experiences are not predictable, and activities are not dependable?

Westerhoff's concern for ceremonial acts, rituals, and ritual acts as significant components of spiritual formation may bring to the minds of some the threat of falling into ritualization. Westerhoff shares that concern and would allay that fear with the encouragement to explain the rituals in the context of instruction. The fear of ritualization must not prevent congregations from providing the rituals and ritual acts that afford children the opportunity to join them in worship. The excitement in the voices of children saying the Lord's Prayer for the first time or singing a portion of the liturgy with the congregation reinforces the fact that as our children worship with the adults of the congregation, they are learning the words and ways of God's people. Indeed, the community's liturgy can be the means whereby children learn the sacred narrative and grow in their identification with this worshiping group. Intentional worship instruction must take place during the school years and be expanded upon during adulthood. The rituals, however, must be done during formation, the earliest years of a child's life.

CHAPTER 4

Planning from a
Child's Perspective

Peter M. Becker

As was noted in the initial chapter in this book, the third component of the *Children in Worship: Study One* was personal interviews with the primary worship planner in the study congregations (see Appendix D). This study visited 100 congregations in the three major Lutheran denominations in eleven locations across the United States. The interviews with the primary worship planner were conducted by the Research Assistant who visited each respective congregation.

This chapter will focus on the following three areas included in the interview schedule:

- importance of involvement of children to the planner and the congregation;
- consideration of children in both typical and special services;
- involvement of school children in worship.

Responses were received from ninety-two worship planners, of which seventy-six (82.6%) were pastors. In response to the question "Who else participates in planning worship" the ninety who responded indicated forty-eight (53.3%) Directors/Ministers of Music were involved; thirty-eight (42.2%) involved other pastors; thirty-five (38.9%) mentioned organists; and thirty-two (35.6%) indicated members of a worship committee/board participated in planning.

Table Eleven reports the differences that were noted among the three Lutheran denominations as to use of others in the worship planning process.

Planner	LCMS	ELCA	WELS
Music Director	55.6% (30)	53.8% (14)	40.0% (4)
Organist	38.9% (21)	30.8% (8)	60.0% (6)
Worship Comm.	27.8% (15)	50.0% (13)	40.0% (4)
Total N	54	26	10

Table Eleven. Additional Worship Planners by Denomination

Use of a worship committee was highest among ELCA respondents (50.0%) and lowest among LCMS respondents (27.8%). WELS respondents indicated the organist as the most frequent planning support; ELCA used the organist least (30.8%). Music directors were more present in both the LCMS and ELCA (55.6% and 53.8%, respectively) than in WELS congregations. The reader will note that in each column the total is more than 100%. In most cases, respondents cited more than one individual or group that was used in worship planning.

Planner	Both	Only School	Only ECC	Neither
Music Director	63.2% (24)	37.5% (3)	60.0% (9)	41.7% (10)
Organist	42.1% (16)	37.5% (3)	26.7% (4)	41.7% (10)
Worship Comm.	36.8% (14)	50.0% (4)	20.0% (3)	41.7% (10)
Total N	38	8	15	10

Table Twelve. Additional Planners by Presence of Schools and/or Early Childhood Centers

Table Twelve presents the impact of the presence of schools and/or early childhood centers. Worship committees were most involved in the sites that had only a school, but music directors were involved least. Organists were found least involved in the settings where only an early childhood center was present.

Importance of the Child's Perspective

One of the questions in the interview measured the respondent's view as to the importance of the child's perspective in the planning of worship. Table Thirteen reports the findings by denomination.

Importance	LCMS	ELCA	WELS
Very	31.0% (18)	38.5% (10)	30.0% (3)
Somewhat	55.2% (32)	61.5% (16)	40.0% (4)
Slightly	10.3% (6)	0.0% (0)	30.0% (3)
None	3.4% (2)	0.0% (0)	0.0% (0)
Total N	58	26	10

Table Thirteen. Importance of the Child's Perspective to Respondent by Denomination

What is surprising is not that one-third of respondents said considering the child's perspective is very important in planning worship, but that two-thirds did not. The ELCA respondents viewed the child's perspective as more important than either LCMS or WELS respondents. Thirty percent of the WELS respondents stated they believed that the child's perspective was only "Slightly Important." Shockingly, two LCMS respondents stated that the child's perspective was of "No Importance."

When looking at the impact of the presence or absence of schools and early childhood centers, an interesting pattern of responses emerges (Table Fourteen). It appears that those who plan worship at congregations with only early childhood centers indicated the highest importance of considering a child's perspective in planning worship. One can only speculate that these congregations have a large proportion of young families and therefore exert

Importance	Both	Only School	Only ECC	Neither
Very	32.4% (12)	37.5% (3)	46.7% (7)	32.1% (9)
Somewhat	59.5% (22)	37.5% (3)	46.7% (7)	57.1% (16)
Slightly	8.1% (3)	25.0% (2)	0.0% (0)	10.7% (3)
None	0.0% (0)	0.0% (0)	6.7% (1)	0.0% (0)
Total N	37	8	15	28

Table Fourteen. Importance of the Child's Perspective to Respondent by Presence of School and/or Early Childhood Center

pressure for inclusion of children in worship.

It is interesting to note that those locations with only a school were least inclined to see high importance for consideration of a child's perspective in worship. In an age of increasing early childhood education and daycare for children in both the public and private sectors, may the presence of a "school only" suggest a more traditional stance toward children's place regarding the home, church, and school?

The respondents at those sites with "both" schools and early childhood centers and those with "neither" fell somewhere in between the other categories in giving importance to the perspective of children in planning worship. One may only speculate whether the importance of schools in LCMS and WELS "permits" less attention to children in worship. Also, "mature" congregations continue to maintain schools, but do not have sufficient "push" from the membership to provide early childhood education and/or daycare. On the other hand, those congregations with only early childhood programs tend to be either "new" congregations or congregations with a "new" and younger membership where there is pressure for involvement of their children in all aspects of their lives, including worship. This conclusion was supported by findings from the focus groups with parents of young children conducted as part of the AAL-supported Church Membership Initiative (Becker, 1993).

Inclusion in Typical Worship Services

The worship planner was asked to indicate what evidence that children and their perspective are being considered could be found in a typical worship service. Ninety-one separate responses represent the wide range of activities viewed as efforts to include children in worship. However, only six activities were reported by ten or more percent of the responses. Table Fifteen reports these items by denomination.

Activity	LCMS	ELCA	WELS	Total
Children's message	69.0% (40)	64.0% (16)	10.0% (1)	61.3% (57)
Children's songs	41.4% (24)	8.0% (2)	30.0% (3)	31.2% (29)
Children's bulletin	34.5% (20)	32.0% (8)	0.0% (0)	30.1% (28)
Communion blsng.	27.6% (16)	40.0% (10)	0.0% (0)	28.0% (26)
Children's choir	17.2% (10)	36.0% (9)	0.0% (0)	20.4% (19)
Stories in sermon	15.5% (9)	0.0% (0)	20.0% (2)	11.8% (11)

N = 93

Table Fifteen. Evidence of Inclusion of Children's Perspective by Denomination

It is apparent that differences exist between the denominations. It appears that the WELS congregations' means of inclusion did not include several strategies popular in both LCMS and ELCA congregations. No WELS worship planner reported using children's bulletins or blessing children at the communion rail. In fact, only children's songs and stories in the sermon were noted more than once.

More ELCA congregations reported use of the children's choirs and communion blessings than did the other two denominations. LCMS congregations included children's songs more often than the other two bodies. Two-thirds of ELCA and LCMS congregations had children's sermons and/or messages and about one-third of them used children's bulletins.

Table Sixteen shows that about two-thirds of those congregations with schools and/or early childhood centers did have a children's message, while

Activity	Both	Only School	Only ECC	Neither
Children's message	68.4% (26)	62.5% (5)	60.0% (9)	48.1% (13)
Children's songs	36.8% (14)	12.5% (1)	46.7% (7)	18.5% (5)
Children's bulletin	26.3% (10)	12.5% (1)	26.7% (4)	37.0% (10)
Communion blsng.	23.8% (9)	25.0% (2)	26.7% (4)	29.6% (8)
Children's choir	23.7% (9)	37.5% (3)	13.3% (2)	18.5% (5)
Stories in sermon	15.8% (6)	37.5% (3)	13.3% (2)	0.0% (0)
N = 88	38	8	15	27

Table Sixteen. Evidence of Inclusion by Presence of School and/or Early Childhood Center.

slightly less than one-half of those with neither did. It appears that the presence of an early childhood program—either with a school or alone—also increases the presence of both children's messages and children's songs. The presence of a school increased the likelihood of a children's choir in the worship service. The presence of only a school increased the likelihood of the use of stories in the sermon. Two other observations appear to be of interest. First, the presence or absence of schools and early childhood centers had little impact on the percentages of congregations that blessed children during communion. About one-fourth of congregations observed this practice.

The other item of interest is the use of children's bulletins. Use was highest—about one-third—among those congregations that had neither a school nor a center. It was lowest in those congregations that had only a school—about one-eighth. One quarter of those places that had an early childhood program used the children's bulletin. Again, this may indicate a pattern of some locations using bulletins for children since they need any source of contact with children, while those longer established locations with only a school have more traditional approaches, not special bulletins for children.

An additional question probed the frequency of involvement in given types of participation by those less than eighteen years old. Its inclusion is based on the research team's belief that greater involvement leads to greater identification and formation. Table Seventeen reports these findings.

Festival/Activity	Weekly	Monthly	Annually	Never	N
Acolytes	81.1% (77)	2.1% (2)	1.1% (1)	15.8% (15)	95
Bearers	17.9% (15)	9.5% (8)	44.1% (37)	28.6% (24)	84
Readers	4.5% (4)	25.0% (22)	42.0% (37)	28.4% (25)	88
Ushers	33.3% (30)	37.8% (34)	13.3% (12)	15.6% (14)	90
Choir	34.8% (31)	49.4% (44)	12.4% (11)	3.4% (3)	89

Table Seventeen. Participation in Typical Services by Children under Eighteen

For those under the age of majority, participation in worship is primarily supportive. Frequently mentioned ways of worshiping included lighting candles weekly, ushering periodically, and bearing crosses, candles, and Bibles on festival Sundays.

The only two direct means of participation in the actual conduct of worship are choirs and, far less frequently, reading scriptures. Children and/or youth choirs participate at least monthly in about one-half of the congregations and weekly in another one-third. This is the prime mode of participation across congregations. Reading is done mostly in "special" situations for 42% of the congregations. An additional three-tenths use non-adult readers at least monthly.

Perhaps the best way to look at types of participation by denomination is to look at those who "never" have children participating in the worship activity listed. Table Eighteen reports that data.

Activity	LCMS	ELCA	WELS
Acolytes	6.9% (4)	3.8% (1)	90.9% (10)
Bearers	18.9% (9)	17.4% (4)	100.0% (11)
Readers	25.9% (14)	13.0% (3)	72.7% (8)
Ushers	16.4% (9)	8.3% (2)	27.3% (3)
Choir	5.5% (3)	0.0% (0)	0.0% (0)
N = 90	55	24	11

Table Eighteen. Children Under Eighteen Never Participating by Denomination

It appears that participation that brings children into the chancel is less common in WELS congregations than in those of the ELCA and LCMS.

Table Nineteen suggests an interesting observation. While it may be a function of the non-random sample used in this study, it is intriguing that those settings with a school but no early childhood center had the highest rate of never letting children serve as acolytes, bearers, or readers.

Activity	Both	Only School	Only ECC	Neither	N
Acolytes	15.8% (6)	37.5% (3)	7.1% (1)	13.8% (4)	89
Bearers	23.5% (8)	42.9% (3)	15.4% (2)	40.0% (10)	79
Readers	31.4% (11)	50.0% (4)	28.6% (4)	20.0% (5)	82
Ushers	26.5% (9)	14.3% (1)	13.3% (2)	7.1% (2)	84
Choir	0.0% (0)	0.0% (0)	16.7% (2)	3.6% (1)	84

Table Nineteen. Under Eighteen Non-Participation by Presence of School and/or ECC

Those with neither education agency had less participation as bearers, but more participation as acolytes and readers. Those with both educational agencies have the overall highest participation rate. It appears that, for some, tradition—and perhaps theology—mitigates against children's participation.

Special Services

Moving from the typical worship service, the worship planners were asked to indicate the extent of children's participation in special services. It was assumed that children might experience greater participation in "special" worship services. Table Twenty reports the findings.

Clearly, the church festival days involve planned inclusion of children in the services. Christmas and Easter especially involve children. And the Christmas Sunday School program is almost universal among the congregations who reported children's participation in special services. It was far more common than even day school involvement. However, with the emphasis on involvement on special holidays, is it surprising that there are

Activity	Always	Sometimes	Rarely	Never	N
Christmas:					
day school only	66.7% (28)	16.7% (7)	2.4% (1)	14.3% (6)	42
sunday schl only	89.3% (75)	6.0% (5)	3.6% (3)	1.2% (1)	84
combined	46.7% (21)	8.9% (4)	8.9% (4)	35.6% (16)	45
Advent	27.2% (22)	35.8% (29)	13.6% (11)	23.5% (19)	81
Lent	26.4% (23)	42.5% (37)	9.2% (8)	21.8% (19)	87
Holy Week	31.8% (27)	34.1% (29)	12.9% (11)	21.2% (18)	85
Easter	60.2% (56)	17.2% (56)	8.6% (8)	14.0% (13)	93
Youth	49.2% (42)	17.6% (15)	5.9% (5)	27.1% (23)	85
Scout	20.0% (13)	12.3% (8)	18.5% (12)	49.2% (32)	65

Table Twenty: Children's Involvement in Special Services

many people who become "Christmas and Easter" worshipers?

Youth involvement in special services was found in about three of four reporting congregations. It appears that youth services are established in many congregations.

Scout recognition services never occurred in half the reporting congregations. It should be noted one-third of the congregations did not respond to this question, probably because scouting was not an activity found in their settings.

Finally, it is noteworthy that about two-thirds of the congregations that had schools and/or early childhood centers had a school service, and about one-half also had joint services with the Sunday School children.

The differences noted by denomination were few for involvement in Advent, Christmas, and Easter services with one exception. A lower percent of WELS congregations involved children in Easter services.

As might be expected, WELS congregations did not have scouting services, and also had lower participation with drama services and youth services.

Differences by the presence of educational agencies were as expected: those with schools had the highest participation; those with the early childhood centers slightly less; and those with neither had the least participation. What this suggests is that the time it takes to work with children for participation in special services is more readily available to those who have children in full-time education settings. Additionally, involvement with parents, and especially with parents of younger children, may provide subtle pressure for children's involvement.

School Services

The final focus of this chapter is chapel worship services. It was the assumption of the research team that school services would provide an opportunity for greater involvement in worship. Table Twenty-One clearly indicates much higher participation of children in a larger variety of worship functions. Participation in the expressive forms (art, music, and drama), in liturgical aspects such a reading texts and leading worship; and in support roles such as acolyte, bearer and usher allow children to be in worship, not just observing adults doing worship for them.

Activity	Weekly	Monthly	Festival	Rarely/Never	N
Acolytes	62.2% (28)	0.0% (0)	4.4% (4)	33.3% (15)	45
Bearers	20.9% (9)	0.0% (0)	20.9% (9)	58.1% (25)	43
Read text	24.4% (11)	22.2% (10)	17.8% (8)	35.6% (16)	45
Ushers	57.8% (26)	8.9% (4)	6.7% (3)	26.7% (12)	45
Choir	42.2% (19)	33.3% (15)	15.5% (7)	8.9% (4)	45
Musician	15.9% (7)	20.5% (9)	34.1% (15)	29.5% (13)	44
Drama	6.5% (3)	37.0% (17)	34.8% (16)	21.7% (10)	46
Art work	6.7% (3)	22.2% (10)	46.7% (21)	45.5% (11)	45
Lead worship	9.1% (4)	22.7% (10)	22.7% (10)	45.5% (20)	44

Table Twenty-One: School Children's Involvement in Worship

The percent differences (Tables Nineteen through Twenty-One) between participation in school services and in typical congregational worship raise several questions. First, why can children be viewed as providing leadership roles in school chapel settings, but be excluded from sharing their insights with adults? From a child's perspective, wouldn't one feel somewhat alienated from the weekly worship service where one can only be an observer rather than a true participant and leader?

A second question that is implicit involves the extent to which both genders are involved in school chapel settings, as compared to the weekly worship services. While not directly addressed in this interview schedule, the authors have all noted the greater involvement of women and girls in school chapels as compared to weekly worship services. This question will be probed in a future study planned by CenSCED.

A third issue concerns the "limbo" a child may face between active participation in worship while in elementary school and far lower participation in congregational worship as a teen. Is it any wonder that in a series of group interviews done with over 200 Lutheran high school students, weekly worship in their home congregations was reported as "boring" by the overwhelming majority? (Becker & Becker, 1996).

Table Twenty-Two reports the percentages of congregations with Lutheran schools and/or early childhood centers that report various forms of worship participation in school chapel/worship services.

Activity	LCMS	ELCA	WELS	N
Acolytes	68.8% (22)	60.0% (3)	37.5% (3)	45
Bearers	23.3% (7)	40.0% (2)	0.0% (0)	43
Read text	59.4% (10)	40.0% (2)	0.0% (0)	45
Ushers	68.8% (22)	60.0% (3)	62.5% (5)	45
Choir	81.3% (26)	60.0% (3)	62.5% (5)	45
Musician	31.2% (10)	50.0% (2)	50.0% (4)	44
Drama	46.9% (15)	50.0% (3)	25.0% (2)	46
Art work	25.8% (8)	50.0% (3)	25.0% (2)	45
Lead worship	43.8% (14)	0.0% (0)	0.0% (0)	44

Table Twenty-Two: School Children's Involvement in Worship by Denomination—At Least Monthly

WELS educational centers report somewhat lower overall participation of children in worship than the other two denominations. None of the educational centers have children reading the lessons or leading worship.

LCMS and ELCA educational centers are quite similar, with one notable exception. Almost half of the LCMS centers note that children lead worship at least once a month. This clearly suggests that children are viewed as capable, with direction, of sharing their faith in the worship setting. It will be intriguing to explore in future work of CenSCED, school children's perception of peers in the leadership role.

Implications of the Findings

While worship planners feel that some attention should be given to inclusion of children in the worship life of the congregation, evidence suggests that only the children's message is a widely found form of inclusion. An obvious question is, how well are the children's messages reaching children? Anecdotal comments from the research associates indicate that many well-intentioned children's messages are just not developmentally appropriate for children. Since this is the major vehicle for involvement of children, attention should be given to aiding those delivering the children's message in making them as appropriate as possible.

Involvement in other capacities during the service appears to be limited to supporting roles for many. In light of the much different experience found in school and/or early childhood center chapel services, it may be asked if the older child may in fact find school chapels more fulfilling and worshipful than Sunday morning worship. This issue will be explored in a future study in the *Children in Worship* project.

Finally, children's involvement in special services appears to be highest during the traditional Christmas and Easter seasons. While that involvement should be encouraged, a serious question arises. What is the consequence for the rest of the church year and children's involvement? This practice may even lead to some believing those seasons are the only significant seasons of the church. The potential impact of that perspective on the development of "Christmas and Easter" worshipers needs to be explored.

CHAPTER 5

Lessons from Research

Shirley K. Morgenthaler

For the church, the topic of worship, and especially children in worship, has merely begun to be explored. In most congregations, according to the recently completed Study One of the *Children in Worship* (CIW) project, children are taken for granted and are almost invisible. Congregations rarely use an "impact on children" index when considering new programs or congregational policies. For most leaders in the church, children belong to members. Yet the Lutheran understanding of baptism would indicate otherwise. Children are members!

The task of studying children in worship and the congregation's role in enriching that worship has just begun. More work is needed. Plans for such work are underway at CenSCED. Study Two of *Children in Worship* is already proposed and has received initial funding for the planning phase of the study. The completed Study One is descriptive, identifying what current practices, attitudes, and environments exist in Lutheran congregations across the United States. This baseline study is critical to future work and provides the foundation for continued understanding of the impact of con-gregational practice on children in worship.

As a result of the work of Study One, it has become apparent that three separate but related contexts impact children's understanding of, and involvement in, worship. Through interviews with worship planners, it has become apparent that, in addition to the study of corporate worship as the context for children in worship, worship in schools and early childhood centers also needs to be studied. Furthermore, worship at home in the family setting is a context which needs to be studied and understood if children's understandings of worship activities and meanings are to be fully compre-hended.

Corporate Worship

This initial study of CIW has looked primarily at the corporate worship set-ting. The decision to limit the study in this manner has emerged from the theoretical framework of John Westerhoff (1976, 1982, 1992). His perspec-tive on faith formation has provided a seminal paradigm for considering the development of the child's experience and understanding of the faith into which he/she has been baptized.

Westerhoff's work on the social context of faith formation was first out-lined in *Will our Children Have Faith?* (Westerhoff, 1976). It is that corpo-rate context which must be understood if congregations hope to address the needs of children in the planning and implementation of worship as the gathered people of God.

Shared Meanings

For worship to have its full power of meaning for the Christian, whatever the age of that Christian, its meaning must be understood. While worship has power beyond the understanding of any Christian simply because it is sacra-mental (God to people) as well as sacrificial (people to God), understanding its meanings and symbols enriches the worship of the individual of any age.

For children, the issue of shared meanings is particularly important. In all of learning, concept development is dependent on meanings and ideas which are shared and refined in that sharing. Through their experiences, children develop conceptualizations, or individual and idiosyncratic ideas of experiences, rituals, and symbols. Only as those experiences, rituals, and symbols are shared through discussion and definition, do children's conceptualizations develop into the concepts and shared meanings of the community of faith.

For children, the shared meanings of corporate worship need to be experienced and explored within the context of that worship. They need to know the meaning of the cross and of the candles. They need to be told the reason for prayer and confession. They need to understand the elements of worship and their importance to the historic and ongoing telling of the faith story.

The Power of Ritual

Liturgy is ritual. It is the repeated and repetitious telling of the faith story so that all understand. For children, this means the predictable points of participation to which they can look forward from Sunday to Sunday are important. For all Christians, this shared ritual is powerful beyond the immediate experience as a way of communicating their membership in the church universal.

For liturgy to be predictable for children, it must have an element of sameness and structure. While this sameness can be dynamic, it needs to contain sameness to be accessible to the child (and to the visitor or new Christian).

For children, the opportunity to participate in prayers by folding hands and kneeling is a powerful point of entry into liturgy. So, too, the exchange of peace and making the sign of the cross. These acts become children's early entry into the liturgy of the Church. For many children, the presence of familiar versicles and responses sung by the congregation is an opportunity for participation. For the non-reading child, the opportunity to participate in liturgy is solely dependent on the presence of those predictable elements.

While adults and older children can follow a new or creative liturgical pattern, young children cannot. If they are to be considered as members whose needs, too, are to be served, then liturgy must be predictable. The absence of some of the historic elements of the liturgy in many of the churches surveyed indicates to the CIW team that children's needs may not fully be served by the diminution of ritual and predictability in those worship services.

The Power of Environment

Appropriate worship environments for young children teach children about worship. Are there visual images of faith and faith stories for children to see and study? Are there symbols which depict the key elements of the faith of the worshiping community? Are there objects to touch which tell the faith story? Are there sounds which appeal to and can be understood by young children? Are there smells and aromas which signify "church" and "worship" for the child? Each of the senses can potentially be used by the child to learn more about the faith story of the worshiping community.

Appointments in the environment may quickly indicate whether young children are even expected to be or to stay in the worship setting. The attitude of welcome on the part of the congregation is measured by families with young children by the small but powerful messages the environment gives. These environmental messages of welcome may include the presence of booster seats and children's bulletins. They may also include the presence of a children's bulletin board that displays children's "church art." These welcoming messages also include an observation of where in the sanctuary families with young children tend to sit. Can young children participate visually in the worship?

In fully 10% of the congregations visited in the CIW study, a cross – the centerpiece of the Christian theology of substitutionary atonement – was not present. What is the environment saying to children in that case? How can elements of the faith speak to children nonverbally if they are not there?

The Power of Planning

The intentionality of experiences provided for children are also important. Children learn most powerfully and effectively when adults provide experiences which take the child's capacity to comprehend into account. For children, this means that there are regular patterns of participation which can be remembered and understood. It also means that there is a frequency of participation beyond the "high holiday" approach to including children in worship.

The "psychological visibility" of children in the planning process is critical if the full power of planning for children in worship is to be experienced. This would seem to indicate the need for an active concern for children's perspectives and comprehension of worship events. Children sense when they are considered important by adults. They know when they are being ignored or taken for granted. They are fully aware whether they are visible or invisible in the congregational context.

The Power of Participation

Yet another factor to be considered in children's corporate worship experience is the presence of an early childhood education center as a part of the congregation's ministry to children. Congregations offering early childhood programs as a part of their ministry (with or without the presence of a full elementary school) appeared to provide a greater range of participatory experiences for children in corporate Sunday morning worship. This is not to be confused with weekday chapel experiences which were also a part of the offerings in most of these congregations. Study One of CIW looked only at corporate weekend worship experiences and their provision for children's participation.

It is the conclusion of the researchers that the presence of early childhood weekday programming, both with an elementary school and in freestanding centers, was a strong indicator of greater participation and "visibility" of children in corporate worship. Was the visibility of children during the week the cause of greater provision for children on the weekend? Or was the provision for children on the weekend a motivator to find ways to also provide programming for young children during the week? More research will be needed to answer these questions. However, the lower levels of participation for children in worship in settings with only elementary schools (and no early childhood education component) or with no formal weekday education enterprise would seem to indicate that children were not as great a concern in these settings.

Recommendations—Worship Rituals

Worship rituals which support and extend children's participation unto understanding of worship will include predictable elements which children will recognize each week. These elements need to include:

- prayers and prayer postures
- the exchange of peace in which children are intentionally greeted
- the sign of the cross, made by congregation as well as clergy
- specific addresses to children in the sermon of the day
- responsive liturgy which is predictably present so that it will be learned by children

The children's sermon is a worship element which must be used to teach children, not the adults who are "listening in." For children, this means opportunities to hear the worship experience explained in language they can understand. This includes:

- explorations of the symbolic and theological significance of elements of the environment, such as the cross, the candles, and the baptismal font
- explanations of pieces of the liturgy in a series of children's sermons
- discussion of the parament colors and their meanings
- consideration of the banners, windows, and icons in the environment and of their meanings
- discussion of "words to listen for" in the main sermon which will encourage attention to that message
- exhortations to tell others the good news of Jesus as child evangelists

Recommendations—Worship Environments

Church environments which are planned with children in mind will "speak" to the pre-literate child in powerful ways through the visual images of color and symbol. They will also "speak" to the child through auditory messages beyond words, such as through bells, language cadences, and loud/soft sounds.

These aspects indicate whether worship is considered an adult or an intergenerational activity. These aspects also indicate whether children are expected to learn to worship by worshiping. The analysis of the CIW Study One results indicates that, for most children, worship is a spectator activity. This is due, at least in part, to the messages of the environment.

Positive messages which welcome children and their families include:

- realistic banners which communicate the faith story to young children
- physical provisions for children, such as booster seats and "church bags"
- explanations of the environment from a liturgic standpoint
- references to changes in the liturgic environment so that children can understand their meaning
- seating expectations which assure that children can see the focus of worship and begin to participate more fully

Recommendations—Planning

Planning for the inclusion of children in worship needs to include the intentional planning of a pattern of participation which will be experienced by children. It also involves assuring the inclusion of role models who, by their participation, communicate the message that children, too, can aspire to participation. This is especially important for the regular and frequent inclusion of adolescents as acolytes, ushers, and readers. Younger children will be more likely to interpret the participation of youth as "accessible" than that of adults or clergy.

Worship planning also needs to include the intentional provision for worship education. While some of this worship education may be placed in the children's sermon, other outside-of-worship time needs to be planned for such experiences.

Specific recommendations for worship planning include:

- intentional planning for frequent participation of pre-confirmation children in worship activities
- planning for messages of welcome, both verbal and nonverbal, to fami-

lies with young children

- utilizing school-age children as acolytes and assistant ushers
- providing for role models of varying ages in worship leadership; also attending to questions of gender and ethnic diversity as possible
- planning for bulletin and/or newsletter inserts which sensitize congregational members to the children in worship
- providing intentional accommodations for young children that give messages that they are expected in worship (such as booster seats, front-row reserved seating, a "children's corner" bulletin board, etc.)

Conclusions and Implications

From the data reported in the previous four chapters in this volume, it is clear that the perspective of children in worship was not strongly considered in the majority of the congregations included in the study. Yet, if Westerhoff's theory (1992, 1996) is valid, these congregations have missed an important opportunity.

The opportunity to welcome children into worship begins with small but powerful messages that children are expected to be present. These messages would include where children are expected to be seated if they are to participate, whether special seating accommodations, such as booster chairs for toddlers and preschoolers, are available, and what kinds of other intentional provisions have been made for children and their families.

From the perspective of the worship ritual, the messages of welcome include specific references to children in the main sermon, whether or not a children's sermon is also present. It includes intentional greetings to children on the part of the pastor and parishioners. It includes predictability of liturgy which children can follow and are intentionally taught.

From the perspective of planning, worship planners need first of all to consider that children are members from the moment of their baptism. As members, they deserve the same consideration as members of other ages. Not greater consideration, but the same attention and regard.

Questions to Consider

As congregations consider the importance of including children in worship there are key questions which can inform and guide that consideration.

1. What are we doing for worship education? Can "field trips" to the sanctuary be planned for Saturday morning family outings?

2. Do we "celebrate" or "perform" worship? What are the evidences of each in the weekly worship of this congregation?

3. What is the appropriate movement from "formation" to "instruction" for the children in this congregation? Are we giving them enough affective experiences on which to base their cognitive understandings?

4. How and when do we articulate the shared meanings of the elements of worship? How and when are the rituals and practices explained even to adults?

5. How and when are children allowed and encouraged to explore the worship environment? Would that Saturday morning field trip help them to feel comfortable in the environment?

6. Do the banners we display include real enough representations for young children to understand? Are the meanings of abstract banners ever explained?

7. Do we have icons and artifacts of the essential tenets of Lutheran theology (e.g., cross, Trinity, key Bible stories, etc.)?

8. Do we display symbols and signs of the church year to remind both children and adults of the faith story we celebrate?

9. Do we consider the participation of children in worship to "mess up" worship for adults?

10. If we have a school or early childhood center in our congregation, what is the relationship of congregational worship to the life of that educational and/or caregiving enterprise? How is the ministry of the entire congregation carried out in the schooling of children?

11. If we do not have a school or early childhood center, what are we doing to intentionally reach out to children and their families through the worship practices of this congregation?

12. Do we encourage the participation of members of all ages, both individually and as groups, in the corporate worship of this congregation?

13. How are children welcomed into the worshiping community?

14. What accommodations are made and/or available for families with young children?

15. Are young children being taught to tune out before they have even tuned in?

16. What are the messages of welcome which would tell children and their parents that they are not simply tolerated, but welcomed and provided for?

Each congregation will need to assess its accommodations for and welcoming of children for itself. Each congregation will need to determine if there are practices and attitudes which can be modified in order to move worship for children from a "spectator activity" to a meaningful experience in which children, too, can celebrate their relationship with God and grow in that relationship.

Closing Thoughts

In many congregations, worship appears to be a performance rather than a celebration. Lutheran theology regards worship as a sacrificial and sacramental celebration of God's story of love and redemption. Worshipers of all ages need to understand that dynamic.

If congregations are to truly include worshipers of all ages, they need to provide for the needs and perspectives of those varying age levels. For children, this means that children need to be encouraged to worship, even if their form of participation is noisier or more boisterous than that of the adult. It means that congregations need to structure worship so that children's participation and style of participation are included and valued. It means considering children's participation valuable and important, not a disruption to the worship of adults.

The environmental elements of worship, such as changing colors, changing paraments, banners, even wreaths and Easter crosses, need to be explained. Children, especially, need to know what the environment and the liturgy of a given Sunday or season of the church year are teaching. However, it is quite possible that the reason children do not know the significance of elements of worship is that their parents also do not know!

Church leaders, worship planners, and parents all bear responsibility for providing appropriate access for children in the worship setting. Families of young children receive messages of welcome and accommodation (or the lack thereof) from the small ways in which accommodations for children are made in the environment, the planning, and the worship itself. In addition, children and their families receive messages of welcome or non-welcome from the attitudes caught through glances or comments in response to the wiggles or noises of a young child.

If Westerhoff's theory is correct, as the researchers believe, then Lutheranism must reexamine its worship practices in regard to children. In Westerhoff's theory, children are not to be relegated to a children's church or a "developmentally appropriate experience." Rather, they are to be welcomed into a truly intergenerational worship experience in which both the setting and the worship rituals themselves are planned with believers of all ages in mind.

It is incumbent upon church leaders to examine the value for children of corporate worship as it is currently practiced.

AFTERWORD

If the observation is true that all research is ultimately "subjective," the work reported in this book was indeed subjective research. Although the methodologies employed mirrored those used in current empirical research, the selection of the topic and the careful analysis of the results were not the results of detached, objective reflection. As is evident in the reports, this subject is dear to the hearts of the CenSCED research team.

As grandparents motivated by a concern for the spiritual well-being of their grandchildren, the authors devoted time and energy to the tasks involved. As Lutheran ministers motivated by the Lord's concern for the spiritual life of children, the authors viewed their work as being of great potential value for Lutheran parents, teachers, and pastors. As such, this book is offered to the Church as an act of service motivated by the love of children and the love of Christ.

The promise made by parents and sponsors at the baptism of a child includes the pledge " . . . to bring the child to the services of God's house." This first study of the CIW research project was designed to collect data on what is happening in the "services of God's house," and how children experience those services. As the CIW project continues in Studies Two and Three, attention will be given to understanding how children participate in and perceive the worship experience. Children and their families will be observed in the worship context, with attention to the kinds and degrees of participation. Subsequently, children will be given the opportunity to share their perceptions of the worship activities of their faith community through interviews and/or by "playing church."

All phases of the *CIW* research project will be conducted according to current research practices. However, the motivation for each activity will be to assist parents and those charged with the spiritual care of children in fulfilling their most important task. That task is the spiritual formation of the child, to the end that the child may " . . . grow up to lead a godly life to the praise and honor of Jesus Christ."

Gary L. Bertels

REFERENCES

Becker, P. M. (1993). *Why non-churched parents do or do not join Lutheran churches.* River Forest, IL: Concordia University, CenSRCH Research Report.

Becker, P. M. & Becker, E. M. (1996). *The affective domain in Lutheran high school religious instruction.* River Forest, IL: Concordia University, CenSRCH Research Report.

Morgenthaler, S. K. (Ed.). (1999). *Exploring children's spiritual formation: Foundational issues.* River Forest, IL: Pillars Press.

Piaget, J. (1955). *The language and thought of the child.* New York: Meridian Books.

Sperry, W. (1932). *Reality in worship.* New York: Macmillan.

Westerhoff, J. H. (1976). *Will our children have faith?* New York: Seabury Press.

Westerhoff, J. H. (1980). *Bringing up children in the Christian faith.* Minneapolis, MN: Winston Press.

Westerhoff, J. H. (1992). The school of the church: Fashioning Christians in our day. In S. A. Hauerwas & J. H. Westerhoff (Eds.), *Schooling Christians: "Holy experiments" in American education* (pp. 262 - 281). Grand Rapids, MI: Eerdmans.

Westerhoff, J. H. (1996, May). *Living into baptism.* Paper presented at a pre-conference session of the Lutheran Education Association Convocation, Detroit, MI.

Westerhoff, J. H. (1997). Lutheran schools and the making of Christians. *Lutheran Education, 133,* 5-12.

APPENDIX A

List of Congregations

Ascension Evangelical Lutheran Church
2820 12th Avenue S.
Moorehead, MN 56560

Ascension Lutheran Church
1440 SE 182nd Avenue
Portland, OR 97233-5009

Atonement Evangelical
Lutheran Church
4500 N. Sherman Boulevard
Milwaukee, WI 53209

Austin Messiah Lutheran Church
908 N. Waller Avenue
Chicago, IL 60651-2695

Beautiful Savior Lutheran Church
9800 SE 92nd Avenue
Portland, OR 97266

Beautiful Savior Lutheran Church
12513 E. Mill Plain Boulevard
Vancouver, WA 98684

Beautiful Savior Lutheran Church
3210 Maple Drive
PO Box 336
Plover, WI 54467-0336

Bethany Lutheran Church
1550 Modaff Road
Naperville, IL 60565

Bethel Lutheran Church
130 N. Keeler
Chicago, IL 60624

Bethel Lutheran Church
1410 N. Springfield Avenue
Chicago, IL 60651

Bethlehem Lutheran Church
655 Forest Street
St. Paul, MN 55106-4508

Bethlehem Lutheran Church
2153 Salisbury Street
St. Louis, MO 63107

Bethlehem Lutheran Church
PO Box 249
Crete, NE 68333

Bethlehem Lutheran Church
18865 SW Johnson Street
Aloha, OR 97006-3164

Bloomington Lutheran Church
9350 Portland Avenue S.
Bloomington, MN 55420

Calvary Lutheran Church
5321 W. McFadden Avenue
Santa Ana, CA 92704

Calvary Lutheran Church
1750 N. Calhoun Road
Brookfield, WI 53005

Canoga Park Lutheran Church
7357 Jordan Avenue
Canoga Park, CA 91303

Christ the Lord Lutheran Church
1650 N. Brookfield Road
Brookfield, WI 53045

Christ Lutheran Church
2475 E. 17th Avenue
North St. Paul, MN 55109

Christ Lutheran Church
223 E. 5th Street
Zumbrota, MN 55992

Christ Our Savior Lutheran Church
14175 Farmington Road
Livonia, MI 48154

Concordia Lutheran Church
505 S. Kirkwood Road
Kirkwood, MO 63122

Cross Lutheran Church
1821 N. 16th Street
Milwaukee, WI 53205

Cross View Lutheran Church
6645 McCauley Trail
Edina, MN 55439-1074

Darlington Lutheran Church
3545 Packard Road
Ann Arbor, MI 48105

Divine Shepherd Lutheran Church
2600 Nexon Road
Ann Arbor, MI 48105

Emmanuel Lutheran Church
Ninth & Beaver
York, NE 68467

Emmaus Lutheran Church
5215 Loop Road
Dorsey, IL 62021

Epiphany Chandler Lutheran Church
800 W. Ray
Rond Chandler, AZ 85224

Epiphany Lutheran Church
PO Box 309
Arlington, AL 36722-0309

Epiphany Lutheran Church
810 E. South Boulevard
Montgomery, AL 36116-2308

Faith Lutheran Church
1703 Martin L. King Avenue
Mobile, AL 36617

Faith Lutheran Church
856 W. Eldredge
Pocatello, ID 83201

Faith Lutheran Church
8300 S. Sangamon Street
Chicago, IL 60620-3138

Faith Lutheran Church
5911 Telegraph Road
St. Louis, MO 63129

Faith Lutheran Church
6345 Madison Avenue
Lincoln, NE 68507

Faith Lutheran Church
1245 N. 2nd Street
Seward, NE 68434

Faith Lutheran Church
12th & Ohio
York, NE 68467

Family in Faith Christian Church
1480 Bloomingdale Road
Glendale Heights, IL 60139

First Immanuel Lutheran Church
W67 N622 Evergreen Boulevard
Cedarburg, WI 53012-1848

Fishers of Men Lutheran Church
2011 Austin Parkway
Sugarland, TX 77479

Gethsemane Lutheran Church
2723 Orange Avenue
La Crescenta, CA 91214-2124

Good Shepherd Lutheran Church
620 Second Street
PO Box 90
Milford, NE 68405

Children In Worship

Grace Lutheran Church
1350 Baldy Avenue
Pocatello, ID 83201

Grace Lutheran Church
252 N. 6th Street
Seward, NE 68434

Grace Lutheran Church
7610 NE Fremont
Portland, OR 97213

Holy Cross Lutheran Church
3110 N. Hayden Road
Scottsdale, AZ 85251

Holy Cross Lutheran Church
13014 Olive Boulevard
Creve Coeur, MO 63141-6152

Holy Family Lutheran Church
542 W. Hobbie Street
Chicago, IL 60610

Holy Savior Lutheran Church
4710 N. 10th Street
Lincoln, NE 68521

Holy Word Lutheran Church
10601 Bluff Bend
Austin, TX 78753

Immanuel Lutheran Church
2055 Filer Avenue E.
Twin Falls, ID 83301

Immanuel Lutheran Church
142 E. Third Street
Elmhurst, IL 60126

Immanuel Lutheran Church
1505 W Michigan Avenue
Jachson, MI 49202

Immanuel Lutheran Church
317 W. Pearce Boulevard
Wentzville, MO 63385

King of Kings Lutheran Church
13765 Olive Boulevard
Chesterfield, MO 63017

King of Kings Lutheran Church
17000 N 620 Smyers Lane
Round Rock, TX 78681

Lord of Life Lutheran Church
15750 Baxter Road
Chesterfield, MO 63017

Lutheran Church of Atonement
1285 New Florissant Road N.
Florissant, MO 63031

Lutheran Church of the Good Shepherd
1500 6th Street S.
Moorehead, MN 56560

Lutheran Church of the Savior
3616 East G Avenue
Kalamazoo, MI 69004

Martin Luther Memorial Church
4219 NE Martin Luther King Boulevard
Portland, OR 97211

Messiah Lutheran Church
2846 S. Grand Boulevard
St. Louis, MO 63118

Messiah Lutheran Church
1800 S. 84th Street
Lincoln, NE 68506

Our Redeemer Lutheran Church
1000 14th Street S.
Moorehead, MN 56560

70

Our Redeemer Lutheran Church
2508 Gull Road
Kalamazoo, MI 49001

Our Redeemer Lutheran Church
3743 Marysville Road
Staplehurst, NE 68439-8843

Our Savior Lutheran Church
1513 E. Yager Lane
Austin, TX 78753

Peace Lutheran Church
6145 Maple Avenue
PO Box 123
Sussex, WI 53089-0123

Pilgrim Lutheran Church
3257 E. University Drive
Mesa, AZ 85213

Prince of Peace Lutheran Church
37775 Palmer Road
Westland, MI 48186

Redeemer Lutheran Church
510 S. 33rd Street
Lincoln, NE 68510

Redeemer Lutheran Church
795 E. Powell Boulevard
Gresham, OR 97030-7615

Redeemer Lutheran Church
1500 W. Anderson Lane
Austin, TX 78757

Redhill Lutheran Church
13200 Redhill Avenue
Tustin, CA 92680-3839

Reformation Lutheran Church
2201 N. 35th Street
Milwaukee, WI 53208

Resurrection Lutheran Church
7400 August Street
River Forest, IL 60305

Resurrection Lutheran Church
1700 NE 132nd Avenue
Portland, OR 97230

St. James Lutheran Church
2046 N. Fremont Street
Chicago, IL 60614

St. John Lutheran Church
154 S. Shaffer Street
Orange, CA 92866

St. John Lutheran Church
305 Circle Avenue
Forest Park, IL 60130

St. John Lutheran Church
505 S. Park Road
La Grange, IL 60525

St. John Lutheran Church
35320 Glenwood
Westland, MI 48186

St. John Lutheran Church
919 N. Columbia Avenue
Seward, NE 68434

St. John Lutheran Church
14746 Sanford Avenue
Flushing, NY 11355

St. John Lutheran Church
Fenimore Road & Cortland Avenue
Mamaroneck, NY 10543

St. John Lutheran Church
2885 Division Road
Jackson, WI 53037

St. Luke Lutheran Church
4205 Washtenaw Avenue
Ann Arbor, MI 48108

St. Luke Lutheran Church
95 Eastchester Road
New Rochele, NY 10801

St. Mark Lutheran Church
6337 Clayton Road
St. Louis, MO 63117-1808

St. Mark Lutheran Church
27 St. Mark's Place
Yonkers, NY 10704

St. Martin Lutheran Church
000 W. 15 Street
Austin, TX 78701

St. Martini Lutheran Church
1520 S. 16th Street
Milwaukee, WI 53204-2715

St. Matthew Lutheran Church
5402 Wren Avenue
St. Louis, MO 63120-2442

St. Paul Lutheran Church
132 Sixth Avenue South
Birmingham, AL 35205-4227

St. Paul Lutheran Church
4475 Atlanta Highway
Montgomery, AL 36109

St. Paul Lutheran Church - Agoura Hills
30600 Thousand Oaks Boulevard
Agoura Hills, CA 91301

St. Paul Lutheran Church
555 E. Benton Street
Aurora, IL 60505

St. Paul Lutheran Church
420 W. Liberty Street
Ann Arbor, MI 48103

St. Paul Lutheran Church
100 W. 6th Street
Jordan, MN 55352

St. Paul Lutheran Church
PO Box 398
Utica, NE 68456

St. Paul Lutheran Church
3501 Red River Street
Austin, TX 78705

St. Paul Lutheran Church
610 Fowzer Street
Taylor, TX 76574

St. Paul Lutheran Church
W 1955 Gopherhill Road
Ixonia, WI 53036

St. Paul Lutheran Church
16 S. Walnut Street
Mayville, WI 53050-1557

St. Peter Lutheran Church
1510 N. Parton Street
Santa Ana, CA 92706

St. Philip Lutheran Church
9745 Bissonnet Street
Houston, TX 77036

St. Thomas Holy Spirit Lutheran Church
3980 S. Lindbergh Boulevard
St. Louis, MO 63127-0581

Trinity First Lutheran Church
1115 E. 19th Street
Minneapolis, MN 55404-2035

Trinity Lutheran Church
446 S. Gay Street
Auburn, AL 36830-5937

Trinity Lutheran Church
2668 Berkley Avenue
Mobile, AL 36617-1704

Trinity Lutheran Church
1104 Rosa L. Parks Avenue
Montgomery, AL 36108

Trinity Lutheran Church
1900 Range Street
Selma, AL 36703

Trinity Lutheran Church
902 S. Broadway
Santa Ana, CA 92701

Trinity Lutheran Church
405 S. Rush Street
Roselle, IL 60172

Trinity Lutheran Church
1400 W. Stadium Boulevard
Ann Arbor, MI 48103

Trinity Lutheran Church
504 South Westnedge Avenue
Kalamazoo, MI 49007-5054

Trinity Lutheran Church
167 Palisade Avenue
Bogota, NJ 07603

Trinity Lutheran Church
3610 S. Highway 95
PO Box 72
Taylor, TX 76574

Village Lutheran Church
9237 Clayton Road
Ladue, MO 63124

The Village Lutheran Church
172 White Plains Road
Bronxville, NY 10708

Zion Lutheran Church
1501 W. Liberty Street
Ann Arbor, MI 48103

Zion Lutheran Church
2122 Bronson Boulevard
Kalamazoo, MI 49008

Zion Lutheran Church
784 Jackson Street
St. Paul, MN 55117

Environment Checklist

<table>
<tr><td colspan="2">Congregation name</td></tr>
</table>

CenSCED
Concordia University
River Forest, Illinois

city/state/zip

Observer

C.I.W. - Environment Checklist

Please circle a response for each item.

A. Architecture

1. Exterior
   a. Warmness/Coldness   5   4   3   2   1
   b. Openness/Closedness   5   4   3   2   1
   c. Accessibility to children   5   4   3   2   1
2. Interior
   a. Warmness/Coldness   5   4   3   2   1
   b. Openness/Closedness   5   4   3   2   1
   c. Place to walk w/ restless toddlers   5   4   3   2   1
   d. Accessibility to children   5   4   3   2   1

B. Chancel appointments
(Also indicate the location of each appointment on the Sanctuary diagram)

1. Communion rail presence   Y   N
2. Pulpit presence   Y   N
3. Lectern presence   Y   N
4. Baptismal font presence   Y   N
5. Crucifix presence   Y   N
6. Paraments presence   Y   N
7. Altar presence   Y   N
8. Candles
   a. Altar   Y   N
   b. Communion   Y   N
   c. Baptism   Y   N
   d. Eternal light   Y   N

C. Sensory components

1. Heat: warm/adequate/cool   W   A   C
2. Light: bright/adequate/dim   B   A   D
3. Sound:
   a. clear/adequate/muffled   C   A   M
   b. loud/moderate/soft   L   M   S

- 1 -

4. Smell (strong=3/moderate=2 /absent=1)

a. Candles	3	2	1
b. Incense	3	2	1
c. Wood	3	2	1
d. Flowers	3	2	1
e. Other_____	3	2	1

D. Nave appointments

1. Unobstructed sight lines to altar	5	4	3	2	1
2. Reserved area for families w/ young children	front		none		back
3. Kneelers				Y	N
4. Booster seats available				Y	N
5. Banners					
a. Present				Y	N
b. Primarily words				Y	N
c. Words and symbols				Y	N
d. Symbols and pictures				Y	N
6. Baptismal font					
a. Prominence	5	4	3	2	1
b. Font location:					
Chancel				Y	N
Narthex				Y	N
Other_____				Y	N

(please specify)

E. Iconic representations

1. Easily viewable by children	5	4	3	2	1
2. Stained glass				Y	N
3. Murals				Y	N
4. Pictures/paintings				Y	N
5. Statues				Y	N
6. Ecclesiastical vestments					
a. Cassock/Surplice				Y	N
b. Alb				Y	N
c. Chasuble				Y	N
7. Content of representations					
a. Jesus				Y	N
b. Trinity				Y	N
c. Prominent Bible stories				Y	N
d. Saints				Y	N
e. Non-specific designs				Y	N
f. Abstract art				Y	N

- 2 -

F. Balcony

1. Presence
   - None   =   1
   - Rear Only   =   2
   - Side(s) Only   =   3
   - Rear and Side(s)   =   4
2. Access
   - None   =   1
   - Congregation Only =   2
   - Musicians Only   =   3
   - Both   =   4

G. Narthex

1. Size
   - None   =.   1
   - Cramped   =   2
   - Adequate   =   3
   - Spacious   =   4
2. Appointments

a. Coat Racks/Rooms	Y	N
b. Mail Boxes	Y	N
c. Tract Racks	Y	N
d. Visuals	Y	N
e. Other:_____	Y	N

(Please list)

H. Musical elements

1. Presence

a. Organ	Y	N
b. Piano	Y	N
c. Bells	Y	N
d. Other instruments	Y	N
e. Choir loft	Y	N

2. Location (Balcony=1/Chancel=2/Nave=3)

a. Organ	1	2	3
b. Piano	1	2	3
c. Bells	1	2	3
d. Other instruments	1	2	3
e. Choir loft	1	2	3

APPENDIX C

Worship Checklist

Children In Worship

CenSCED
Concordia University
River Forest, Illinois

city/state/zip

Observer

"Children in Worship"
Worship Checklist

Please circle a response for each item.

	Week 1	Week 2	Week 3
A. Ceremonial Acts			
1. Children's message	Y N	Y N	Y N
2. Children's song	Y N	Y N	Y N
3. Adult leader greeting children	Y N	Y N	Y N
4. Children brought to communion rail	Y N	Y N	Y N
5. Children named in prayers:			
a. Sickness	Y N	Y N	Y N
b. Baptism	Y N	Y N	Y N
c. Baptism birthday	Y N	Y N	Y N
d. Birthday	Y N	Y N	Y N
e. Special needs	Y N	Y N	Y N
f. Accomplishments	Y N	Y N	Y N
g. other_____	Y N	Y N	Y N
6. Comments to children during message	Y N	Y N	Y N
7. Special accommodations for children:			
a. Bulletins-children	Y N	Y N	Y N
b. Seating-reserved	Y N	Y N	Y N
c. Booster seats	Y N	Y N	Y N
d. Nursery	Y N	Y N	Y N
e. Other_____	Y N	Y N	Y N
8. Children involved in worship activities:			
a. Choir	Y N	Y N	Y N
b. Ushering	Y N	Y N	Y N
c. Presenting gifts	Y N	Y N	Y N
d. Speaking	Y N	Y N	Y N
e. Acolyte	Y N	Y N	Y N
f. Crucifer	Y N	Y N	Y N
g. Book bearer	Y N	Y N	Y N
h. Instrumentalists	Y N	Y N	Y N
i. Banner bearer	Y N	Y N	Y N
j. Hand bells	Y N	Y N	Y N
k. Drama group	Y N	Y N	Y N

- 1 -

B. Rituals

	Y N	Y N	Y N
1. Processional			
If Yes - Participants:			
a. Children	Y N	Y N	Y N
b. Clergy	Y N	Y N	Y N
c. Lay Ministers	Y N	Y N	Y N
d. Choir	Y N	Y N	Y N
2. Kneeling for confession	Y N	Y N	Y N
3. Kneeling for Prayer	Y N	Y N	Y N
4. Standing appropriately	Y N	Y N	Y N
5. Child making the sign of the cross	Y N	Y N	Y N
6. Pastor making sign of the cross	Y N	Y N	Y N
7. Gospel procession	Y N	Y N	Y N
If Yes - Participants:			
a. Clergy	Y N	Y N	Y N
b. Acolyte	Y N	Y N	Y N
c. Book Bearer	Y N	Y N	Y N
d. Torch Bearer	Y N	Y N	Y N
8. Holy communion celebrated			
If Yes - Eucharistic assistants:			
a. Gender	F M	F M	F M
b. Race (white/other)	WHBAO	WHBAO	WHBAO
9. Lay readers (Scripture readings):			
a. Gender	F M	F M	F M
b. Race	WHBAO	WHBAO	WHBAO
10. Lay speakers (other than reader):			
a. Gender	F M	F M	F M
b. Race	WHBAO	WHBAO	WHBAO
11. Lay Cantor:			
a. Gender	F M	F M	F M
b. Race	WHBAO	WHBAO	WHBAO
12. Use of hymnal for:			
a. Liturgy	Y N	Y N	Y N
b. Psalm	Y N	Y N	Y N
c. Hymns	Y N	Y N	Y N
d. Catechism	Y N	Y N	Y N
e. Prayers	Y N	Y N	Y N
13. Use of Bible	Y N	Y N	Y N
14. Use of Worship Folder	Y N	Y N	Y N

- 2 -

81

C. Ritual Acts

1. Tolling of the bell	Y N	Y N	Y N
2. Greeting	Y N	Y N	Y N
3. Call to Worship	Y N	Y N	Y N
4. Processional	Y N	Y N	Y N
5. Opening hymn	Y N	Y N	Y N
6. Invocation	Y N	Y N	Y N
7. Confession & Absolution	Y N	Y N	Y N
8. Baptism	Y N	Y N	Y N
9. Entrance rite:			
a. Introit	Y N	Y N	Y N
b. Hymn	Y N	Y N	Y N
10. Kyrie (Lord Have Mercy)	Y N	Y N	Y N
11. Hymn of Praise (Glory to God or This Is the Feast)	Y N	Y N	Y N
12. Collect	Y N	Y N	Y N
13. Bidding Prayer	Y N	Y N	Y N
14. Readings	Y N	Y N	Y N
15. Psalmody	Y N	Y N	Y N
16. Sermon	Y N	Y N	Y N
17. Creed	Y N	Y N	Y N
18. Offering	Y N	Y N	Y N
19. Offertory	Y N	Y N	Y N
20. Preface & Proper Preface	Y N	Y N	Y N
21. Sanctus	Y N	Y N	Y N
22. Lord's Prayer	Y N	Y N	Y N
23. Words of Institution	Y N	Y N	Y N
24. Exchange of Peace:			
a. Spoken only	Y N	Y N	Y N
b. Hand shake	Y N	Y N	Y N
25. Agnus Dei	Y N	Y N	Y N
26. Salutation	Y N	Y N	Y N
27. Benediction	Y N	Y N	Y N
28. Closing Hymn	Y N	Y N	Y N
29. Bell/Chimes	Y N	Y N	Y N
30. Recessional	Y N	Y N	Y N

- 3 -

D. Special Rites

Please indicate if any special rites occurred, such as: induction of workers, confirmation, reception of new members.

Week One: _____

_____

Week Two: _____

_____

Week Three: _____

_____

E. Please submit any worship folders, bulletins, children's materials distributed at the services observed.

Thank you for your assistance in Censced's Children in Worship Project.

Interviewer: _____
(please print)

Dates: Week 1:___/___/___ Week 2:___/___/___ Week 3:___/___/___

Professional Worker
Questionnaire

CenSCED

Concordia University
River Forest, IL

"Children in Worship"
Professional Worker Questionnaire

Introductory Remarks

> *Thank you for agreeing to participate in this research project of the Center for the Study of Children's Ethical Development (CenSCED).*

> *Please answer the questions from your perspective, not those of others in the congregation.*

A. Intentionality

1. Please indicate the degree of importance you give to the child's perspective in the planning of worship.

Very important	___4
Somewhat important	___3
Slightly important	___2
Not important or considered	___1

2. Please indicate who else participates in planning worship:
   e.g. organist, teachers, choir director, worship committee, etc.

_____

_____

> *If the response to A.1 was "very", "somewhat", or "slightly" important, continue with A.3. If the response was "not", SKIP to question A.4.*

- 1 -

3. Put yourself in the place of a child. List evidence in your typical worship service that a child's perspective is being considered.

_____

_____

_____

_____

_____

_____

4. How important to members of the congregation do you feel consideration of the child's perspective is in planning worship?

Very Important	___4
Somewhat Important	___3
Slightly Important	___2
Not important or considered	___1

B. Specific Items

1. Are children invited to come forward for a children's message?

Every service	___7
Weekly, each service	___6
Weekly, at least one service	___5
On alternative Sundays	___4
At least once a month	___3
Occasionally	___2
Never	___1

- 2 -

2. Are children from the family invited to join parents during a baptism?

Always	___4
Frequently	___3
Seldom	___2
Never	___1

3. Are children of the congregation invited to join the family during a baptism?

Always	___4
Frequently	___3
Seldom	___2
Never	___1

4. To what extent are children (under 18) participants in a typical worship service?

Activity	Weekly	Monthly	Festival Only	Annually	Never
a. Acolytes	___	___	___	___	___
b. Bearers	___	___	___	___	___
c. Read Texts	___	___	___	___	___
d. Announcements	___	___	___	___	___
e. Ushers	___	___	___	___	___
f. Choir	___	___	___	___	___
g. Other:_____ (specify)	___	___	___	___	___

- 3 -

5.a. Check the appropriate blank for the amount of specific children's involvement in special worship services.

	<u>Always</u>	<u>Sometimes</u>	<u>Rarely</u>	<u>Never</u>
Advent	____	____	____	____
Christmas:				
S. S.	____	____	____	____
Day school	____	____	____	____
Combined	____	____	____	____
Lent	____	____	____	____
Holy Week	____	____	____	____
Easter	____	____	____	____
Confirmation	____	____	____	____
V. B. S.	____	____	____	____
Youth services	____	____	____	____
Scout services	____	____	____	____
Chancel Drama	____	____	____	____

5.b. Children's participation in special worship services:

_____

_____

_____

_____

_____

- 4 -

6. In a typical worship service, what is the age range for each of the activities listed? (e.g. 6-13, 12-17)

Activity	Lowest	Highest	Does Not Apply
a. Acolytes	___	___	___
b. Bearers	___	___	___
c. Readers	___	___	___
d. Speakers	___	___	___
e. Ushers	___	___	___
f. Choir	___	___	___
g. Other:_____ (specify)	___	___	___

C. Communion/Confirmation Practices

1. Describe your practice regarding young children accompanying parents to the communion rail.

   a. Do they join parents?   Yes___   No___

   b. Do they receive Blessing?   Yes___   No___

   c. Do they receive the Elements? Yes___   No___

2. Describe your first communion/confirmation practices. Indicate age of first communion, confirmation age, and types and length of preparation for both.

   _____

   _____

   _____

   _____

- 5 -

D. Other Inclusion of Children in Worship

1. Please check the frequency of the following means for including children in worship.

Activity	Weekly	At Least Monthly	When Requested	Never
a. Prayer when ill	—	—	—	—
b. Birth	—	—	—	—
c. Baptismal birthday	—	—	—	—
d. Birthday	—	—	—	—
e. Accomplishments	—	—	—	—
f. Special needs	—	—	—	—
g. Ex Corde Prayers	—	—	—	—
h. Prayer Cards	—	—	—	—
i. Other:_____ (specify)	—	—	—	—

2. Please indicate the extent and ways children's songs and/or music are used in worship.

Activity	Always	Sometimes	Rarely	Never
a. Prelude	—	—	—	—
b. Taught in Service	—	—	—	—
c. Interlude	—	—	—	—
d. Postlude	—	—	—	—
e. Led by Child(ren)	—	—	—	—
f. Childrens Choir	—	—	—	—

- 6 -

91

3. Please indicate any other ways you (your congregation) attempt to include children and their perspectives and needs into your worship activities.

_____

_____

_____

_____

_____

> If the church has a school, ask the questions in section E.

> If it does not have a school, go directly to section F.

E. School Chapel/Worship Services

1. To what extent do school children perform the functions listed below in a school chapel/worship service?

Activity	Weekly	Monthly	Festival Only	Rarely	Never
a. Acolytes	—	—	—	—	—
b. Bearers	—	—	—	—	—
c. Read Text	—	—	—	—	—
d. Announcement	—	—	—	—	—
e. Ushers	—	—	—	—	—
f. Choir	—	—	—	—	—
g. Musician	—	—	—	—	—
h. Drama	—	—	—	—	—
i. Art work	—	—	—	—	—
j. Lead worship	—	—	—	—	—
k. Other:_____ (specify)	—	—	—	—	—

- 7 -

2. Please check the frequency of the following means of including children in school chapel/worship.

Activity	Weekly	At Least Monthly	When Requested	Never
a. Prayer when ill	___	___	___	___
b. Birth	___	___	___	___
c. Baptismal birthday	___	___	___	___
d. Birthday	___	___	___	___
e. Accomplishments	___	___	___	___
f. Special needs	___	___	___	___
g. Other:_____ (specify)	___	___	___	___

F. Congregational Information

1. Total (Baptized) Membership   ___ ___ ___ ___

2. Full (Confirmed) Membership   ___ ___ ___ ___

3. Ave. Weekly Worship Attendance   ___ ___ ___ ___

4. Children under 14 in Sunday School   ___ ___ ___

5. Children in School/Early Childhood   ___ ___ ___

6. Number of Regularly Scheduled Services Per Week   _____

List: Days	Time	Type
_____	_____	_____
_____	_____	_____
_____	_____	_____
_____	_____	_____
_____	_____	_____
_____	_____	_____

- 8 -

7 Describe Liturgical Style Preferred

> *Ask the respondent to describe the congregation's style(s) of worship. You may use prompts like: highly liturgical, semi-liturgical, informal, diverse.*

_____

_____

_____

8. Indicate Hymnal(s) used:

    a. Lutheran Worship (LW)

    b. Lutheran Book of Worship (LBW) ____

    c. The Lutheran Hymnal (TLH) ____

    d. Other:_____ ____
              (please specify)

    e. Other:_____ ____
              (please specify)

    f. Other:_____ ____
              (please specify)

9. Do you print service in a worship folder:

    a. Entire service including hymns ____

    b. Only liturgy, not hymns ____

    c. Only outline and changes ____

    d. No printed worship guide ____

    e. Other _____ ____
              (please specify)

10. Church _____
              (name)   (denomination)

          _____
              (city)   (state)   (zip)

- 9 -

G. Demographics of Respondent

1. Gender: Female___1 Male___2

2. Position: Ordained___1 Commissioned___2 Lay___3

3. Title: _____
   (please specify)

4. Years in current position: ___ ___

H. Comments

> *Ask the respondent if she/he has any other thoughts related to children and worship in that congregation.*

> **Thank she/he for the time and support of CenSCED's efforts.**

Interviewer:_____
             (please print)

Date completed: ____/____/____ Length: _____/_____
                month date year   hours minutes

pmb-0296   pmb/1994